EDUCATION AND PERSONALITY

EDUCATION AND PERSONALITY

Edited by

Dr. S.K. Panneer Selvam
Assistant Professor
Deptt. of Education
Bharathidasan University
Tamil Nadu (India)
&
Dr. R. Dhakshina Murthy
Associate Professor
Deptt. of Social Exclusion & Inclusive Policy
Bharathidasan University
Tamil Nadu (India)

DISCOVERY PUBLISHING HOUSE PVT. LTD.
NEW DELHI-110 002

Published by:
Tilak Wasan
DISCOVERY PUBLISHING HOUSE PVT. LTD.
4383/4B, Ansari Road, Darya Ganj
New Delhi-110 002 (India)
Phone : +91-11-23279245, 43596064-65
Fax : +91-11-23253475
E-mail : parul.wasan@gmail.com
discoverypublishinghouse@gmail.com
web : www.discoverypublishinggroup.com

***First Edition:* 2013**

***Reprinted:* 2016**

ISBN: 978-93-5056-254-3

Education and Personality

Printed at:
Infinity Imaging Systems
Delhi

Preface

Personality Type and Managerial Performance Undoubtedly, the personality characteristics influence the performance and this difference among managers can be an important source of difference in managerial effectiveness. There is evidence to support the proposition that the managerial effectiveness is moderated by the personality characteristics. Personality is not easily defined. Basically, 'personality' refers to our attempts to capture or summarize an individual's 'essence'. Personality is personality, the science of describing and understanding persons. Clearly, personality is a core area of study for psychology, if not the core. Together with intelligence, the topic of personality constitutes the most significant area of individual difference study. No two people are exactly the same—not even identical twins. Some people are anxious, some are risk-taking; some are phlegmatic, some highly-strung; some are confident, some shy; and some are quiet and some are loquacious. This issue of differences is fundamental to the study of personality. Note also that in studying these differences we will also examine where the differences come from: as with intelligence we will find that there is a mixture of nature and nurture involved. Personality can be defined as a dynamic and organized set of characteristics possessed by a person that uniquely influences his or her cognitions, motivations, and behaviors in various situations. The word "personality" originates from the Latin *persona,* which means mask. Significantly, in the theatre of the ancient Latin-speaking world, the mask was not used as a plot device to *disguise* the identity of a character, but rather was a convention employed to represent or *typify* that character. The pioneering American psychologist, Gordon Allport (1937) described two major ways to study personality, the nomothetic and the idiographic. *Nomothetic psychology* seeks general laws that can be applied to many different people, such as the principle of self-actualization, or the trait of extraversion. *Idiographic psychology* is an attempt to understand the unique aspects of a particular individual. Psychoanalytic theories explain human behaviour in terms of the interaction of various components of personality. Sigmund Freud was the founder of this school. Freud drew on the physics of his day (thermodynamics) to coin the term psychodynamics. Based on the idea of converting heat into mechanical energy, he proposed psychic energy could be converted into behavior. Freud's theory places central importance on dynamic, unconscious psychological conflicts. Freud divides human personality into three significant components: the id, ego, and super-ego. The *id* acts according to the *pleasure principle,* demanding immediate gratification of its needs regardless of external environment; the *ego* then must emerge in order to realistically meet the wishes and demands of the id in accordance with the outside world, adhering to the *reality principle.* Finally, the *superego* (conscience) inculcates moral judgment and societal rules upon the ego, thus forcing the demands of the id to be met not only realistically but morally. The superego is the last function of the personality to develop, and is the embodiment of parental/social ideals established during childhood. According to Freud, personality is based on the dynamic interactions of these three components. The self is a key construct in several schools of psychology, broadly referring to the cognitive and affective representation of one's identity. The earliest formulation of the self in modern psychology from the distinction between the self as *I,* the subjective knower, and the self as *me,* the object that is known.

Current views of the self in psychology diverge greatly from this early conception, positioning the self as playing an integral part in human motivation, cognition, affect, and social identity. Self following from John Locke has been seen as a product of episodic memory but research upon those with amnesia find they have a coherent sense of self based upon preserved conceptual autobiographical knowledge. It may be the case that we can now usefully attempt to ground experience of self in a neural process with cognitive consequences, which will give us insight into the elements of which the complex multiply situated selves of modern identity are composed. Many early theories suggested that self-esteem is a basic human need or motivation. American psychologist Abraham Maslow, for example, included self-esteem in his hierarchy of needs. He described two different forms of esteem: the need for respect from others and the need for self-respect, or inner self-esteem. Respect from others entails recognition, acceptance, status, and appreciation, and was believed to be more fragile and easily lost than inner self-esteem. According to Maslow, without the fulfillment of the self-esteem need, individuals will be driven to seek it and unable to grow and obtain self-actualization. The originality of this edition owes to the contributors. As an editor we acknowledged to the contributors.

Dr. S.K. Panneer Selvam
Dr. R. Dhakshina Murthy

Contents

Encoding—Channel—Decoding—Receiver—Feedback—Context—Removing Barriers at All These Stages—How to Communicate: Improve Your Relationships with Effective Communication Skills—Interpersonal Relationship—Types—Development—Soft Skills—Examples of Soft Skills—Top 60 Soft Skills—Common Fears of Public Speaking—Why do we get Public Speaking anxiety?—Fight or flight—Why does public speaking do this to us?—How to Overcome Fear of Public Speaking—What good are Nerves—Get your Attention off Yourself—Keep them awake—Public Speaking Training—Get a coach—Focus on positives not negatives—Turn your back on too many rules—You are an individual not a clone—Hints and Tips for Effective Public Speaking—Mistakes—Humour—Tell stories—How to use the public speaking environment—Technology—The 25 Public Speaking Skills Every Speaker Must Have—How to Develop Good Public Speaking Skills—Perception—Types—Assertiveness—Motivation Concepts—Extrinsic Motivation—Self-control—Achievement Motivation—Characteristics of People with a High Need for Achievement—Do People with a High Need for Achievement Behave Like this all the Time?—Rewards and Achievement-motivated People—Feedback—Why do Achievement-motivated People Behave as they do?—Examples—Stress—Types of Stress—Sources of Stress—Personal—Home Stress—Occupational Stress—Society Stress—Natural Stress—Identify the Sources of Stress in your Life—Start a Stress Journal—Look at How you Currently Cope with Stress—Learning Healthier Ways to Manage Stress—Dealing with Stressful Situations: The Four A's—Stress Management Strategy 1: Avoid Unnecessary Stress—Stress Management Strategy 2: Alter the Situation—Stress Management Strategy 3: Adapt to the Stressor—Adjusting Your Attitude—Stress Management Strategy 4: Accept the things you can't Change—

3: Debriefing—Models of Team Behavior—Team Member Qualities—Emotional Stability—Extraversion—Openness—Agreeableness—Organizational Development—Building a New Team—Topchik Identifies 10 Steps for Building a New Project Team —Self-Managed Work Teams—Team Building—Characteristics of Good Team Building—Team Effectiveness—Inside-Out: The Change Starts from Within—The Seven Habits—An Overview—From Dependence to Independence—Habit 1: Be Proactive—Summary of the Habits—Habit 1: Be Proactive—Habit 2: Begin with the End in Mind—Habit 3: Put First Things First—Habit 4: Think Win/Win—Habit 5: Seek First to Understand, Then to Be Understood—Habit 6: Synergize—Habit 7: Sharpen the Saw—Hierarchy of Human Needs—Biography—Humanistic Theories of Self Actualization—Hierarchy of Needs—Writings—Free Team Building Games Training Ideas and Tips—Teamwork—Using and Planning Team-building Activities—Team Exercises and Events for Developing Ethical Organizations—Corporate Events and Social Responsibility—Risks and Dangers of Socially Irresponsible Events and Activities—Excluding Partners from Events...—Tips for Working with Syndicate Groups for Team Building or Training —David c McClelland's Motivational Needs Theory—David McClelland's Needs-based Motivational Model—The Need for Achievement (n-ach)—The Need for Authority and Power (n-pow)—The Need for Affiliation (n-affil)—John Adair's Action Centred Leadership - A Model for Team Leadership and Management—John Adair's Action-centred Leadership Model—Action Centered Leadership and John Adair—Use of John Adair's Action-centred Leadership Ideas, Theories and Diagram—Frederick Herzberg's Motivation and Hygiene Factors—Hertzberg's Main Theory and Its Significance —To what Extent is Money a Motivator?—Douglas

CHAPTER

1

Components of Personality

What Is Personality?

Almost everyday we describe and assess the personalities of the people around us. Whether we realize it or not, these daily musings on how and why people behave as they do are similar to what personality psychologists do. While our informal assessments of personality tend to focus more on individuals, personality psychologists instead use conceptions of personality that can apply to everyone. Personality research has led to the development of a number of theories that help explain how and why certain personality traits develop. While there are many different theories of personality, the first step is to understand exactly what is meant by the term *personality*. A brief definition would be that personality is made up of the characteristic patterns of thoughts, feelings, and behaviors that make a person unique. In addition to this, personality arises from within the individual and remains fairly consistent throughout life. Some of the fundamental characteristics of personality include:

- ***Consistency:*** There is generally a recognizable order and regularity to behaviors. Essentially, people act in the same ways or similar ways in a variety of situations.

- ***Psychological and physiological:*** Personality is a psychological construct, but research suggests that it is also influenced by biological processes and needs.
- ***Impact behaviors and actions:*** Personality does not just influence how we move and respond in our environment; it also *causes* us to act in certain ways.
- ***Multiple expressions:*** Personality is displayed in more than just behavior. It can also be seen in out thoughts, feelings, close relationships, and other social interactions.

Theories of Personality

There are a number of different theories about how personality develops. Different schools of thought in psychology influence many of these theories. Some of these major perspectives on personality include:

- *Type theories* are the early perspectives on personality. These theories suggested that there are a limited number of "personality types" which are related to biological influences.
- *Trait theories* viewed personality as the result of internal characteristics that are genetically based.
- *Psychodynamic theories* of personality are heavily influenced by the work of Sigmund Freud, and emphasize the influence of the unconscious on personality. Psychodynamic theories include Sigmund Freud's psychosexual stage theory and Erik Erikson's stages of psychosocial development.
- Behavioral theories suggest that personality is a result of interaction between the individual and the environment. Behavioral theorists study observable and measurable behaviors, rejecting theories that take internal thoughts and feelings into account. Behavioral theorists include B. F. Skinner and John Watson.

- Humanist theories emphasize the importance of free will and individual experience in the development of personality. Humanist theorists include Carl Rogers and Abraham Maslow.

1. The quality or condition of being a person.
2. The totality of qualities and traits, as of character or behavior, that is peculiar to a specific person.
3. The pattern of collective character, behavioral, temperamental, emotional, and mental traits of a person: *Though their personalities differed, they got along as friends.*
4. Distinctive qualities of a person, especially those distinguishing personal characteristics that make one socially appealing: *won the election more on personality than on capability.* See synonyms at disposition.
   (*a*) A person as the embodiment of distinctive traits of mind and behavior.
   (*b*) A person of prominence or notoriety: *television personalities.*
5. An offensively personal remark. Often used in the plural: *Let's not engage in personalities.*
6. The distinctive characteristics of a place or situation: *furnishings that give a room personality.* What is Personality? Last updated:

Personality is the supreme realization of the innate idiosyncrasy of a living being. It is an act of high courage flung in the face of life, the absolute affirmation of all that constitutes the individual, the most successful adaptation to the universal condition of existence coupled with the greatest possible freedom for self-determination." —Carl Gustav Jung, 1934.

As we Move from Intelligence to Personality...

As this course moves from intelligence (1st 5 weeks) into personality (next 10 weeks), it is worth pointing out that the relationship between intelligence and personality may be stronger than many assume. Intelligence influences different aspects of personality in many different ways. In fact, intelligence is sometimes considered to be part of personality. This issue will probably always be debated. The main point to bear in mind is that both intelligence and personality are prominent individual differences.

Personality is not easily defined. Basically, 'personality' refers to our attempts to capture or summarize an individual's 'essence'. Personality is personality, the science of describing and understanding persons. Clearly, personality is a core area of study for psychology, if not the core. Together with intelligence, the topic of personality constitutes the most significant area of individual difference study. No two people are exactly the same - not even identical twins. Some people are anxious, some are risk-taking; some are phlegmatic, some highly-strung; some are confident, some shy; and some are quiet and some are loquacious. This issue of differences is fundamental to the study of personality. Note also that in studying these differences we will also examine where the differences come from: as with intelligence we will find that there is a mixture of nature and nurture involved.

Perspectives on Personality that we'll be Examining

- Trait Perspective
- Biological Perspective
- Psychoanalytic Perspective
- Learning Perspective
- Phenomenological Perspective
- Cognitive Perspective

Lay Usage of the term "Personality"

We use the term personality frequently but what does it actually mean?

- "She has a wonderful personality."

- "He has no personality." "He has personality plus."
- "We seem to have a personality conflict." "It's just her personality." "She has her mother's personality."
- "He's a real personality."

Personality Comes from the Greek Word "Persona", Meaning "Mask"

The word 'personality' derives from the Latin word 'persona' which means 'mask'. The study of personality can be understood as the study of 'masks' that people wear. These are the personas that people project and display, but also include the inner parts of psychological experience which we collectively call our 'self'.

"I" is for Personality

According to Adams (1954, cited in Schultz & Schultz, 1994) personality is "I". Adams suggested that we get a good idea of what personality is by listening to what we say when we use "I". When you say I, you are, in effect, summing up everything about yourself - your likes and dislikes, fears and virtues, strengths and weaknesses. The word I is what defined you as an individual, as a person separate from all others." (Schultz & Schultz, 1994, p.8)

"I am" Exercise

- Write 10 honest endings to "I am..."
- Share them with someone
- Does this sum up your personality? Why or why not?

Various Definitions of Personality

- "Deceptive masquerade or mimicry."
- "The entire organization of a human being at any stage of development."
- "Levels or layers of dispositions, usually with a unifying or integrative principle at the top."

- "The integration of those systems or habits that represent an individual's characteristic adjustments to the environment."
- "The way, in which the person does such things as remembering, thinking or loving."
- "Those characteristics that account for consistent patterns of behaviour".
- "Personality is not an existing substantive entity to be searched for but a complex constructs to be developed and defined by the observer." (Smith & Vetter, 1982, p. 5)
- A contemporary definition for personality is offered by Carver and Scheier (2000, p. 5): "Personality is a dynamic organisation, inside the person, of psychophysical systems that create a person's characteristic patterns of behaviour, thoughts, and feelings." Carver & Scheier (2000, p. 5)
    - ❑ *Dynamic Organisation:* suggests ongoing readjustments, adaptation to experience, continual upgrading and maintaining Personality doesn't just lie there. It has process and it's organised.
    - ❑ *Inside the Person:* suggests internal storage of patterns, supporting the notion that personality influences behaviours, etc.
    - ❑ *Psychophysical systems:* suggests that the physical is also involved in 'who we are' Characteristic Patterns: implies that consistency/continuity which are uniquely identifying of an individual
    - ❑ *Behaviour, Thoughts, and Feelings:* indicates that personality includes a wide range of psychological experience/manifestation: that personality is displayed in MANY ways.
    - ❑ Carver & Scheier (2000, p.5) suggest that the word personality "conveys a sense of consistency,

internal causality, and personal distinctiveness". This issue of "personal distinctiveness is very important. There are certain universal characteristics of the human race and particular features of individuals. We all for example experience stress and the elevated cortisol that goes with it, and we all suffer the immune suppressive effects thereof. BUT each of us is unique too.

REFERENCES

1. Carver, C. S., & Scheier, M. F. (2000). *Perspectives on Personality* (4th ed.) Boston: Allyn and Bacon.
2. Burger, J. M. (1993). *Personality* (3rd ed.) Pacific Grove, CA: Brooks/Cole.
3. Ridley, M (1999). *Genome: The Autobiography of a Species in 23 chapters.* London: Fourth Estate.
4. Schultz, D., & Schultz, S.E. (1994). *Theories of Personality* (5th ed.) Pacific Grove, CA: Brooks/Cole.

CHAPTER

2

Function of Personality Components

This study tests managerial effectiveness of top and lower level managers in production and marketing departments in relation to their personality type in private sector organisations. A 2×2×2 factorial design was employed, in which there are three independent variables with two levels each: departments (production and marketing), managerial positions (top level and lower level), and personality type (Type A and Type B). Managerial effectiveness is a dependent variable. The main effects of management positions and personality types have been found significant and interaction effects between managerial positions × personality type and among departments × managerial position × personality types have been found significant. The major findings are that in production department, both top and lower level managers having Type B personality are found more effective and in marketing department top-level managers having Type A personality and lower level managers having Type B personality have been found more effective in comparison to their counterparts.

Managerial effectiveness is very important for the survival and growth of the organisation. It is difficult to define managerial effectiveness in concrete terms. Many perceive it within a particular frame of reference. Decisions about effectiveness are bound to be situational and contingent upon the definition and perspectives of those making the judgment. A review of literature shows that managerial effectiveness has been studied with three perspectives:

1. Traditional/Conventional perspective
2. Organisational level competency based perspective, and
3. An individual level competency based perspective.

The traditional model emphasises the ability to set and achieve goals (Bartol and Martin, 1991) where it is implicitly assumed that managerial effectiveness leads to organisational effectiveness.

The organisational competency based approach implies that there is long term future orientation that accounts for both external and internal influences on the organisations. From these analyses a vision is created for the future of the organisation, goals are set that will achieve the vision and plans are developed to achieve these strategic goals. Here, the organisation tries to create the system and environment with the help of skills and characteristics of managers that lead them to achieve strategic intents. The individual competency based approach to managerial effectiveness focuses upon the individual rather than the organisation. The purpose of this approach is to develop transferable (generic) management skills that are applicable across different circumstances both nationally and internationally. But this competency-based perspective on managerial effectiveness has been heavily criticised on the ground of the contingencies and the contexts.

Effectiveness is best seen as something a manager produces from a situation by managing it appropriately, producing the results or meeting the targets in every sphere of the activities of organisations. The manager's job is linked with three major dimensions—technical, conceptual, and human. The productivity of any organisation can be increased by the effective management of all the three dimensions and specially by managing the conceptual and human dimensions of management. All managers need to work with and through subordinates to optimise organisational performance. Therefore, certain behavioural skills are required of individuals if they are to be effective as managers.

Managers have many resources at their disposal and the quality of work is dependent on how well these resources have been used. The performance of a manager can be measured by the extent to which goals that are important to the group and organisations are met through the productive efforts of subordinates (Herbert, 1976). In other words, effective management is the culmination of synergy of effectiveness of individual managers in the organisation (Sen and Saxena, 1999).

Das (1987) identified the characteristics of an efficient branch manager as setting an example by personal qualities, job knowledge, business acumen, and management ability. Miles (1992) suggested that constructive use of authority entails the ability to formulate clear goals and to determine what steps are necessary to achieve them, including getting people to do what is necessary for achieving the targets. Misumi (1989), and Misumi and Peterson (1985) defined the ideal manager in Japan in terms of both performance and maintenance orientations, namely, a manager who leads the group towards goal attainment and preserves its social stability. Just as there had been controversy and many arguments were raised that a good leader should have certain characteristics similar arguments are there for managerial effectiveness. There are many researchers who on the basis of their findings have identified that effective managers possess the particular set of characteristics like job knowledge, good communication, business acumen and interpersonal relationship but having these characteristics are not sufficient to become effective manager. Managerial effectiveness is not only a personality characteristic but it is related to performance and output. Gupta (1996) has developed a 16-factor scale to measure managerial effectiveness. These factors are tapping three important aspects of effectiveness: activities of his position, achieving the results, and developing further potential. The managerial effectiveness has been measured by experts in several different ways at different times. Some models focus on individual competencies of managerial effectiveness, while most of the studies have taken performance measure and superior's appraisals rather than self report measures while deciding the effectiveness of a manager. In the light of above discussion, a study is planned to see the effect of management position, departments, and personality variable on managerial effectiveness.

Personality Type and Managerial Performance Undoubtedly, the personality characteristics influence the performance and this difference among managers can be an important source of difference in managerial effectiveness. There is evidence to support the proposition that the managerial effectiveness is moderated by the personality characteristics. One such variable is Type A versus Type B personality. The types of work environment, level of job position, and personality characteristics are the important variables that affect managerial effectiveness in an organisational environment. This is exactly why personality tests are used in screening of job candidates to avoid potential mismatches. Friedman and Rosenham (1966) defines the Type A personality as "an action emotion complex that can be observed in any person who is aggressively involved in a chronic incessant struggle to achieve more and more in less time and if required to do so, against the opposing efforts of other things or other persons". The Type A personality is characterised by feeling a chronic sense of time urgency and by an excessive competitive drive. Some of the more outstanding characteristics of Type As include:

1. Always in haste

2. Feeling of impatience
3. Obsessed with success
4. Persistent inability to cope with leisure time.
5. Type B personality can be identified by the following characteristics:
6. Never suffer from a sense of time urgency
7. Play for fun and relaxation
8. Can relax without guilt
9. No need to display either their success or accomplishments.

The evidence links these two distinct personality types with diverse behaviours and different performance outcomes depending on the requirements of the job. Finally, there is paucity of studies that establish an effect of personality (Type A and Type B personality profiles) on managerial effectiveness. The second variable, which was taken in the study, is the type of department. Two types of department (marketing and production) were chosen for this purpose. The requirements from these two types of managers are totally different to become effective. The third independent variable selected is the level of the management position.

Two levels of managers (top and lower) participated in the study. The present study is expected to highlight the significance of personality type profile, department, and management position on managerial effectiveness of managers. The hypotheses formulated for the study are:

1. There is a significant difference in managerial effectiveness between managers of the production and marketing departments.
2. There is a significant difference in managerial effectiveness between top and lower level of managers.
3. There is significant difference in managerial effectiveness between managers of Type A and Type B personality profiles.

4. There is significant interaction between departments and managerial positions.
5. There is significant interaction between departments and personality profile.
6. There is significant interaction between managerial positions and personality profile.
7. There is significant interaction among departments, managerial position, and personality profile.

Methodology

Type of Department: Mainly two types of departments (production and marketing) from private organisations were chosen for the study. Duties and responsibilities of both these departments are different from each other. Managers generally are faced with various limitations on their activities, depending on their rank, their role in the organisation, and the kind of organisation they work for. There are differences among the managers of different departments in the amount of time they devote and the type of job they have, the activities of production managers of these organisations will be different from that of marketing managers of the same organisations.

Managerial Levels: There are many different types of managers with diverse tasks and responsibilities.

Top Managers: Composed of a comparatively small group of executives, top management is responsible for overall management of the organisation. It establishes operating policies and guides the organisation's interaction with its environment.

Lower Level Managers: These managers are called first-level managers. First line managers direct operating employees only, they do not supervise other managers. They are foremen or supervisors.

Sample: A sample of 80 managers, all male, from various private sector organisations of western Uttar Pradesh were selected for this study.

Instruments: Managerial Effectiveness Questionnaire (MEQ) developed by Gupta (1996), and Type A-Type B self-test developed by Bortner (1985) were used.

Design of the Study: A 2×2×2 factorial design was used to study the effect of three independent variables (departments, managerial positions, and personality type) on dependent variable (managerial effectiveness).

Procedure: Both the scales were administered on the respondent managers of production and marketing departments while they were on the job. A total of 170 questionnaires (80 in production departments and 90 in marketing departments) were distributed. They were asked to go through the instructions given on the questionnaire and to go ahead as instructed. There is no time limit for completing the tests. The questionnaires were collected from the subjects after completion. Out of 170 subjects, 40 from each department were sorted out. Out of these, 20 subjects were selected from top level managers and 20 from lower level managers in both departments. In both the groups of top and lower level managers, 10 managers were Type A personality and the other 10 were Type B personality in each department.

Scoring and Analysis: The scoring of managerial effectiveness and personality test was according to the instructions given in the manuals.

Results and Discussions: A 2×2×2 analysis of variance was applied to study the effect of two types of department, management position, and personality on managerial effectiveness. The main effects of managerial positions and personality type were found statistically significant on managerial effectiveness. A glance at the table of means shows that top level managers have scored higher (M=195.65) than the lower level managers (M=187.60) on managerial effectiveness. There was a similar trend for personality type. Managers having Type B personality profile were found more effective (M=195.35) in comparison to Type A managers

(M=187.90). Further, for df=1.72, managerial position × personality type interaction effect (F=38.34, $p<0.01$ level) and three-way interaction (department × managerial position × personality) effect was also found to be significant. These results supported the four hypotheses. However, the main effect of department and two-way interactions between D×M and D×P were not found significant at any level of confidence.

The important finding was that the department × managerial position × personality type interaction turned out to be significant (F=5.92; df, 1, 72, $p<0.05$). This suggested that significant managerial position × personality type interaction was not the same for two departments (production and marketing). Type B managers at the top level are more effective in the production department than managers having Type A personality. In the marketing department, managers having Type A personality at the top level are more effective. Similarly, at the lower level, Type B managers are more effective in the production department but in marketing also managers having Type B personality at the lower level are found to be more effective. The means for departments × managerial positions × personality type interaction for managerial effectiveness are presented. This shows that work environment of the departments also plays an important role in the managerial effectiveness of managers having different personality types and placed at different levels of managerial position.

Thus, from the perusal of the findings it appears that managerial effectiveness is related with the managerial position. Top level managers' managerial effectiveness was higher in comparison to lower level managers. The findings of the present study is in line with the Srivastava and Kumar study (1984), which shows that junior level officers were found less effective compared to middle level managers. The possible cause of this difference in effectiveness may be the higher maturity level and longer managerial experience of the middle level officers. Miles (1992) suggested that the constructive use of authority entails the ability to formulate clear goals and to determine what steps are necessary to achieve them, including getting people to do what is required.

In spite of the Type A's hard work, the Type Bs are the ones who appear to make it to the top. Great salespersons are usually Type As; while senior executives are usually Type Bs (Robbins, 1996). Steers (1995) research revealed that in the very top positions Type Bs are more successful than Type As, who are not overly ambitious, are more patient, and take a broader view of life. Studies have revealed that where high energy alone is a major determinant in job success, Type As should be highly effective. For jobs where originality, thought, and care are important, the Type B personality should be more successful. England and Lee (1974), Chakrabarti and Kundu (1984), and Howell et al (1997) found more effective managers as pragmatic, dynamic, warm hearted, attentive, easygoing, persevering, emotionally mature and stable (personality characteristics create the parameters for people's behaviour, they give a framework for predicting behaviour).

Conclusion

The results of the study indicate that management position and personality type are associated with self-perceived managerial effectiveness. As hypothesised top-level managers and Type B managers have been found higher on managerial effectiveness as compared to lower level managers and Type A managers. A three-way interaction among type of department, managerial position, and personality type shows joint effect on managerial effectiveness.

In the selection process, this information regarding an applicant's personality type can enable the employer to make appropriate selection decision thus ensuring match between person and job. It also provides opportunities to identify potentials of suitable employees for higher-level managerial jobs based on their personality types. It will be beneficial both for employees and the organisation. A self-report method has been used to measure the managerial effectiveness. Rating by the superiors and peers, if taken and correlated with it would have given substantive results but mostly fair evaluation by them is not done. Personal bias and rivalry distort the results.

REFERENCES

1. Bartol K and D Martin, 1991. Management. New York: McGraw-Hill.
2. Bortner RW, 1985. "A Short Rating Scale as a Potential Measure of Pattern Behaviour", In Fred Luthans, Organisational Behavior, McGraw-Hill.
3. Chakrabarti PK and R Kundu, 1984. "Personality Profiles of Management Personnel", Psychological Studies, 29.
4. Das GS, 1987. "Conflict Management Styles of Efficient Branch Managers: as Perceived by Others," ASCI Journal of Management, 17(1), 30-38.
5. Ellen van Velsor and Jean Brittain Leslie, 1995. "Why Executives Derail: Perspective across Time and Cultures," Academy of Management Executive, November, 62-72.
6. England GW and R Lee, 1974. "The Relationship between Managerial Values and Managerial Success in the United States, Japan, India and Australia" Journal of Applied Psychology, 59 (4), 411-419.
7. Friedman and Rosenman, 1966. Qustionnaire on Type A and Type B. In RW Bortner, "A Short Rating Scale as a Potential Measure of Pattern A Behavior," Journal of Chronic Diseases, 22, 87-91.
8. Gupta S, 1996. "Managerial Effectiveness: Conceptual Framework and Scale Development," Indian Journal of Industrial Relations, 31(3), 392-409.
9. Herbert TT, 1976. Dimensions of Organisational Behavior, Macmillan Publishing Co Inc.
10. Howell JP, 1997. DE Bowen, PW Dorfman and S Kerr. "Substitutes for Leadership: Effectiveness Alternatives to Ineffective Leadership," In Veccho, RP. (ed.), Leadership: Understanding the Dynamics of Power and Influence an Organisations, University of Notredame Press.

11. Miles Mary, 1992. The Effective Manager: Semi-Tough, McGraw Hill.
12. Misumi J and MF Peterson, 1985. "The Performance Maintenance Theory of Leadership: Review of a Japanese Research Program," Administrative Science Quarterly, 30,198-223.
13. Richard M Steers, 1984. Introduction to Organisational Behavior, 2e, Scott, Foresman, Glenview, p. 518.
14. Robbins SP, 1988. Organisational Behavior: Concept, Controversies and Applications, Prentice Hall of India, Delhi.
15. Sen S and S Saxena, 1999. "Managerial Effectiveness: Managing with a Difference," Personnel Today, 20(2), 5-11.
16. Shermon G. Managerial Effectiveness: The Difficult Question, http://www.jbims.edu/ publications.htm

CHAPTER

3

Personality Development

Personality development is the development of the organized pattern of behaviors and attitudes that makes a person distinctive. Personality development occurs by the ongoing interaction of *temperament,* character, and environment. Personality is what makes a person a unique person, and it is recognizable soon after birth. A child's personality has several components: temperament, environment, and character. Temperament is the set of genetically determined traits that determine the child's approach to the world and how the child learns about the world. There are no genes that specify personality traits, but some genes do control the development of the nervous system, which in turn controls behavior. A second component of personality comes from adaptive patterns related to a child's specific environment. Most psychologists agree that these two factors-temperament and environment-influence the development of a person's personality the most. Temperament, with its dependence on genetic factors, is sometimes referred to as "nature," while the environmental factors are called "nurture."

While there is still controversy as to which factor ranks higher in affecting personality development, all experts agree that high-quality parenting plays a critical role in the development of a child's personality. When parents understand how their child responds to certain situations, they can anticipate issues that might be problematic for their child. They can prepare the child for the situation or in some cases they may avoid a potentially difficult situation altogether. Parents who know how to adapt their parenting approach to the particular temperament of their child can best provide guidance and ensure the successful development of their child's personality. Finally, the third component of personality is character-the set of emotional, cognitive, and behavioral patterns learned from experience that determines how a person thinks, feels, and behaves. A person's character continues to evolve throughout life, although much depends on inborn traits and early experiences. Character is also dependent on a person's *moral development*.

In 1956, psychiatrist Erik Erikson provided an insightful description as to how personality develops based on his extensive experience in psychotherapy with children and adolescents from low, upper, and middle-class backgrounds. According to Erikson, the socialization process of an individual consists of eight phases, each one accompanied by a "psychosocial crisis" that must be solved if the person is to manage the next and subsequent phases satisfactorily. The stages significantly influence personality development, with five of them occurring during infancy, childhood, and *adolescence.*

Personality psychology is a branch of psychology that studies personality and individual differences. Its areas of focus include:

- Constructing a coherent picture of a person and his or her major psychological processes.
- Investigating *individual differences,* that is, how people can differ from one another.
- Investigating human nature, that is, how all people's behaviour is similar?

Personality can be defined as a dynamic and organized set of characteristics possessed by a person that uniquely influences his or her cognitions, motivations, and behaviors in various situations. The word "personality" originates from the Latin *persona,* which means mask. Significantly, in the theatre of the ancient Latin-speaking world, the mask was not used as a plot device to *disguise* the identity of a character, but rather was a convention employed to represent or *typify* that character. The pioneering American psychologist, Gordon Allport (1937) described two major ways to study personality, the nomothetic and the idiographic. *Nomothetic psychology* seeks general laws that can be applied to many different people, such as the principle of self-actualization, or the trait of extraversion. *Idiographic psychology* is an attempt to understand the unique aspects of a particular individual.

The study of personality has a broad and varied history in psychology, with an abundance of theoretical traditions. The major theories include dispositional (trait) perspective, psychodynamic, humanistic, biological, behaviorist and social learning perspective. There is no consensus on the definition of "personality" in psychology. Most researchers and psychologists do not explicitly identify themselves with a certain perspective and often take an eclectic approach. Some research is empirically driven such as the "Big 5" personality model whereas other research emphasizes theory development such as psychodynamics. There is also a substantial emphasis on the applied field of personality testing. In psychological education and training, the study of the nature of personality and its psychological development is usually reviewed as a prerequisite to courses in abnormal or clinical psychology.

Personality Theories

Critics of personality theory claim personality is "plastic" across time, places, moods, and situations. Changes in personality may indeed result from diet (or lack thereof), medical effects, significant events, or learning. However, most personality theories emphasize stability over fluctuation.

Trait Theories

According to the *Diagnostic and Statistical Manual* of the American Psychiatric Association, personality traits are "enduring patterns of perceiving, relating to, and thinking about the environment and oneself that are exhibited in a wide range of social and personal contexts." Theorists generally assume a) traits are relatively stable over time, b) traits differ among individuals (e.g. some people are outgoing while others are reserved), and c) traits influence behavior. The most common models of traits incorporate three to five broad dimensions or factors. The least controversial dimension, observed as far back as the ancient Greeks, is simply extraversion and introversion (outgoing and physical-stimulation-oriented vs. quiet and physical-stimulation-averse).

- *Gordon Allport* delineated different kinds of traits, which he also called dispositions. *Central traits* are basic to an individual's personality, while *secondary traits* are more peripheral. *Common traits* are those recognized within a culture and thus may vary from culture to culture. *Cardinal traits* are those by which an individual may be strongly recognized.
- *Raymond Cattell's* research propagated a two-tiered personality structure with sixteen "primary factors" (16 Personality Factors) and five "secondary factors."
- *Hans Eysenck* believed just three traits-extraversion, neuroticism and psychoticism-were sufficient to describe human personality. Differences between Cattell and Eysenck emerged due to preferences for different forms of factor analysis, with Cattell using oblique, Eysenck orthogonal, rotation to analyse the factors that emerged when personality questionnaires were subjected to statistical analysis. Today, the Big Five factors have the weight of a considerable amount of empirical research behind them, building on the work of Cattell and others.

- *Lewis Goldberg* proposed a five-dimension personality model, nicknamed the "Big Five":
    1. ***Openness to Experience:*** the tendency to be imaginative, independent, and interested in variety vs. practical, conforming, and interested in routine.
    2. ***Conscientiousness:*** the tendency to be organized, careful, and disciplined vs. disorganized, careless, and impulsive.
    3. ***Extraversion:*** the tendency to be sociable, fun-loving, and affectionate vs. retiring, somber, and reserved.
    4. ***Agreeableness:*** the tendency to be softhearted, trusting, and helpful vs. ruthless, suspicious, and uncooperative.
    5. ***Neuroticism:*** the tendency to be calm, secure, and self-satisfied vs. anxious, insecure, and self-pitying.

  The Big Five contain important dimensions of personality. However, some personality researchers argue that this list of major traits is not exhaustive. Some support has been found for two additional factors: excellent/ordinary and evil/decent. However, no definitive conclusions have been established.
- *John L. Holland's RIASEC* vocational model, commonly referred to as the *Holland Codes,* stipulates that six personality traits lead people to choose their career paths. In this circumplex model, the six types are represented as a hexagon, with adjacent types more closely related than those more distant. The model is widely used in vocational counseling.

Trait models have been criticized as being purely descriptive and offering little explanation of the underlying causes of personality. Eysenck's theory, however, does propose biological mechanisms as driving traits, and modern behavior genetics researchers have shown a clear genetic substrate to them. Another potential weakness of trait theories is that they lead people to accept oversimplified classifications, or worse offer advice, based on a superficial analysis of their personality. Finally, trait models often underestimate the effect of specific situations on people's behavior. It is important to remember that traits are statistical generalizations that do not always correspond to an individual's behavior.

Type Theories

Personality type refers to the psychological classification of different types of people. Personality types are distinguished from personality traits, which come in different levels or degrees. For example, according to type theories, there are two types of people, introverts and extraverts. According to trait theories, introversion and extraversion are part of a continuous dimension, with many people in the middle. The idea of psychological types originated in the theoretical work of Carl Jung and William Marston, whose work is reviewed in Dr. Travis Bradberry's *The Personality Code*. Jung's seminal 1921 book on the subject is available in English as *Psychological Types*. Building on the writings and observations of Jung, during World War II, Isabel Briggs Myers and her mother, Katharine C. Briggs, delineated personality types by constructing the Myers-Briggs Type Indicator. This model was later used by David Keirsey with a different understanding from Jung, Briggs and Myers. In the former Soviet Union, Lithuanian Aušra Augustinavièiûtë independently derived a model of personality type from Jung's called Socionics.

The model is an older and more theoretical approach to personality, accepting extraversion and introversion as basic psychological orientations in connection with two pairs of psychological functions:

- Perceiving functions: sensing and intuition (trust in concrete, sensory-oriented facts vs. trust in abstract concepts and imagined possibilities)
- Judging functions: thinking and feeling (basing decisions primarily on logic vs. considering the effect on people).

Briggs and Myers also added another personality dimension to their type indicator to measure whether a person prefers to use a judging or perceiving function when interacting with the external world. Therefore they included questions designed to indicate whether someone wishes to come to conclusions (judgment) or to keep options open (perception). This personality typology has some aspects of a trait theory: it explains people's behaviour in terms of opposite fixed characteristics. In these more traditional models, the sensing/intuition preference is considered the most basic, dividing people into "N" (intuitive) or "S" (sensing) personality types. An "N" is further assumed to be guided either by thinking or feeling, and divided into the "NT" (scientist, engineer) or "NF" (author, humanitarian) temperament. An "S", by contrast, is assumed to be guided more by the judgment/perception axis, and thus divided into the "SJ" (guardian, traditionalist) or "SP" (performer, artisan) temperament. These four are considered basic, with the other two factors in each case (including always extraversion/introversion) less important. Critics of this traditional view have observed that the types can be quite strongly stereotyped by professions (although neither Myers nor Keirsey engaged in such stereotyping in their type descriptions), and thus may arise more from the need to categorize people for purposes of guiding their career choice. This among other objections led to the emergence of the five-factor view, which is less concerned with behavior under work conditions and more concerned with behavior in personal and emotional circumstances. (It should be noted, however, that the MBTI is not designed to measure the "work self," but rather what

Myers and McCaulley called the "shoes-off self.") Some critics have argued for more or fewer dimensions while others have proposed entirely different theories (often assuming different definitions of "personality").

Type A and Type B Personality Theory

During the 1950s, Meyer Friedman and his co-workers defined what they called Type A and Type B behavior patterns. They theorized that intense, hard-driving Type A personalities had a higher risk of coronary disease because they are "stress junkies." Type B people, on the other hand, tended to be relaxed, less competitive, and lower in risk. There was also a Type AB mixed profile. Dr. Redford Williams, cardiologist at Duke University, refuted Friedman's theory that Type A personalities have a higher risk of coronary heart disease; however, current research indicates that only the hostility component of Type A may have health implications. Type A/B theory has been extensively criticized by psychologists because it tends to oversimplify the many dimensions of an individual's personality.

Psychoanalytic Theories

Psychoanalytic theories explain human behaviour in terms of the interaction of various components of personality. Sigmund Freud was the founder of this school. Freud drew on the physics of his day (thermodynamics) to coin the term psychodynamics. Based on the idea of converting heat into mechanical energy, he proposed psychic energy could be converted into behavior. Freud's theory places central importance on dynamic, unconscious psychological conflicts. Freud divides human personality into three significant components: the id, ego, and super-ego. The *id* acts according to the *pleasure principle*, demanding immediate gratification of its needs regardless of external environment; the *ego* then must emerge in order to realistically meet the wishes and demands of the id in accordance with the outside world, adhering to the *reality principle*. Finally, the *superego* (conscience) inculcates moral judgment and societal rules upon the ego, thus forcing the demands of the id to be met not only realistically but morally. The superego is the last function of the personality to develop, and is the embodiment of parental/ social ideals established during childhood. According to Freud, personality is based on the dynamic interactions of these three components.

The channeling and release of sexual (libidal) and aggressive energies, which ensues from the "Eros" (sex; instinctual self-preservation) and "Thanatos" (death; instinctual self-annihilation) drives respectively, are major components of his theory. It is important to note Freud's broad understanding of sexuality included all kinds of pleasurable feelings experienced by the human body. Freud proposed five psychosexual stages of personality development. He believed adult personality is dependent upon early childhood experiences and largely determined by age five. Fixations that develop during the infantile stage contribute to adult personality and behavior.One of Sigmund Freud's earlier associates, Alfred Adler, did agree with Freud early childhood experiences are important to development, and believed birth order may influence personality development. Adler believed the oldest was the one that set high goals to achieve to get the attention they lost back when the younger siblings were born. He believed the middle children were competitive and ambitious possibly so they are able to surpass the first-born's achievements, but were not as much concerned about the glory. Also he believed the last born would be more dependent and sociable but be the baby. He also believed that the only child loves being the center of attention and matures quickly, but in the end fails to become independent.

Heinz Kohut thought similarly to Freud's idea of transference. He used narcissism as a model of how we develop our sense of self. Narcissism is the exaggerated sense of one self in which is believed to exist in order to protect one's low self esteem and sense of worthlessness. Kohut had a significant impact on the field by extending Freud's theory of narcissism and introducing what he called the 'self-object transferences' of mirroring and idealization. In other words, children need to idealize and emotionally "sink into" and identify with the idealized competence of admired figures such as parents or older siblings. They also need to have their self-worth mirrored by these people. These experiences allow them to thereby learn the self-soothing and other skills that are necessary for the development of a healthy sense of self. Another important figure in the world of personality theory was Karen Horney. She is credited with the development of the "real self" and the "ideal self". She believes all people have these two views of their own self. The "real self" is how you really are with regards to personality, values, and morals; but the "ideal self" is a construct you apply to yourself to conform to social and personal norms and goals. Ideal self would be "I can be successful, I am CEO material"; and real self would be "I just work in the mail room, with not much chance of high promotion".

Behaviorist Theories

Behaviorists explain personality in terms of the effects external stimuli have on behavior. It was a radical shift away from Freudian philosophy. This school of thought was developed by B. F. Skinner who put forth a model which emphasized the mutual interaction of the person or "the organism" with its environment. Skinner believed children do bad things because the behavior obtains attention that serves as a reinforcer. For example: a child cries because the child's crying in the past has led to attention. These are the *response,* and *consequences*. The response is the child crying, and the attention that child gets is the reinforcing consequence. According to this theory, people's behavior is formed by processes such as operant conditioning. Skinner put forward a "three term contingency model" which helped promote analysis of behavior based on the "Stimulus - Response - Consequence

Model" in which the critical question is: "Under which circumstances or antecedent 'stimuli' does the organism engage in a particular behavior or 'response', which in turn produces a particular 'consequence'?"

Richard Herrnstein extended this theory by accounting for attitudes and traits. An attitude develops as the response strength (the tendency to respond) in the presences of a group of stimuli become stable. Rather than describing conditionable traits in non-behavioral language, response strength in a given situation accounts for the environmental portion. Herrstein also saw traits as having a large genetic or biological component as do most modern behaviorists.

Ivan Pavlov is another notable influence. He is well known for his classical conditioning experiments involving dogs. These physiological studies led him to discover the foundation of behaviorism as well as classical conditioning.

Social Cognitive Theories

In cognitivism, behavior is explained as guided by cognitions (e.g. expectations) about the world, especially those about other people. Cognitive theories are theories of personality that emphasize cognitive processes such as thinking and judging.

Albert Bandura, a social learning theorist suggested the forces of memory and emotions worked in conjunction with environmental influences. Bandura was known mostly for his "Bobo Doll experiment". During these experiments, Bandura video taped a college student kicking and verbally abusing a bobo doll. He then showed this video to a class of kindergarten children who were getting ready to go out to play. When they entered the play room, they saw bobo dolls, and some hammers. The people observing these children at play saw a group of children beating the doll. He called this study and his findings observational learning, or modeling. Early examples of approaches to cognitive style are listed by Baron (1982). These include Witkin's (1965) work on field dependency, Gardner's (1953) discovering people had consistent preference for the number of categories they used to categorise heterogeneous objects, and Block and Petersen's (1955) work on confidence in line discrimination judgments. Baron relates early development of cognitive approaches of personality to ego psychology. More central to this field have been:

- Self-efficacy work, dealing with confidence people have in abilities to do tasks;
- Locus of control theory dealing with different beliefs people have about whether their worlds are controlled by themselves or external factors;
- Attributional style theory dealing with different ways in which people explain events in their lives. This approach builds upon locus of control, but extends it by stating we also need to consider whether people attribute to stable causes or variable causes, and to global causes or specific causes.

Various scales have been developed to assess both attributional style and locus of control. Locus of control scales include those used by Rotter and later by Duttweiler, the Nowicki and Strickland (1973) Locus of Control Scale for Children and various locus of control scales specifically in the health domain, most famously that of Kenneth Wallston and his colleagues, The Multidimensional Health Locus of Control Scale. Attributional style has been assessed by the Attributional Style Questionnaire, the Expanded Attributional Style Questionnaire, the Attributions Questionnaire, the Real Events Attributional Style Questionnaire and the Attributional Style Assessment Test.

Walter Mischel (1999) has also defended a cognitive approach to personality. His work refers to "Cognitive Affective Units", and considers factors such as encoding of stimuli, affect, goal-setting, and self-regulatory beliefs. The term "Cognitive Affective Units" shows how his approach considers affect as well as cognition.

Personal Construct Psychology (PCP) is a theory of personality developed by the American psychologist George Kelly in the 1950s. From the theory, Kelly derived a psychotherapy approach and also a technique called *The Repertory Grid Interview* that helped his patients to uncover their own "constructs" (defined later) with minimal intervention or interpretation by the therapist. The Repertory Grid was later adapted for various uses within organizations, including decision-making and interpretation of other people's world-views. From his 1963 book, *A Theory of Personality*, pp. 103–104:

- *Fundamental Postulate:* A person's processes are psychologically channelized by the ways in which the person anticipates events.
- *Construction Corollary:* A person anticipates events by construing their replications.
- *Individuality Corollary*: People differ from one another in their construction of events.
- *Organization Corollary:* Each person characteristically evolves, for convenience in anticipating events, a construction system embracing ordinal relationships between constructs.
- *Dichotomy Corollary:* A person's construction system is composed of a finite number of dichotomous constructs.
- *Choice Corollary:* People choose for them selves the particular alternative in a dichotomized construct through which they anticipate the greater possibility for extension and definition of their system.
- *Range Corollary:* A construct is convenient for the anticipation of a finite range of events only.
- *Experience Corollary:* A person's construction system varies as the person successively construes the replication of events.

- *Modulation Corollary:* The variation in a person's construction system is limited by the permeability of the constructs within whose ranges of conveniences the variants life.
- *Fragmentation Corollary:* A person may successively employ a variety of construction subsystems which are inferentially incompatible with each other.
- *Commonality Corollary:* To the extent that one person employs a construction of experience which is similar to that employed by another; the psychological processes of the two individuals are similar to each other.
- *Sociality Corollary:* To the extent that one person construes another's construction processes, that person may play a role in a social process involving the other person.

Humanistic Theories

In humanistic psychology it is emphasized people have free will and they play an active role in determining how they behave. Accordingly, humanistic psychology focuses on subjective experiences of persons as opposed to forced, definitive factors that determine behavior. Abraham Maslow and Carl Rogers were proponents of this view, which is based on the "phenomenal field" theory of Combs and Snygg (1949). Maslow spent much of his time studying what he called "self-actualizing persons", those who are "fulfilling themselves and doing the best they are capable of doing". Maslow believes all who are interested in growth move towards self-actualizing (growth, happiness, satisfaction) views. Many of these people demonstrate a trend in dimensions of their personalities. Characteristics of self-actualizers according to Maslow include the four key dimensions:

1. *Awareness:* maintaining constant enjoyment and awe of life. These individuals often experienced a "peak

experience". He defined a peak experience as an "intensification of any experience to the degree there is a loss or transcendence of self". A peak experience is one in which an individual perceives an expansion of his or herself, and detects a unity and meaningfulness in life. Intense concentration on an activity one is involved in, such as running a marathon, may invoke a peak experience.

2. ***Reality and problem centered***-they have tendency to be concerned with "problems" in their surroundings.
3. ***Acceptance/Spontaneity***-they accept their surroundings and what cannot be changed.
4. ***Unhostile sense of humor/democratic***-they do not like joking about others, which can be viewed as offensive. They have friends of all backgrounds and religions and hold very close friendships.

Maslow and Rogers emphasized a view of the person as an active, creative, experiencing human being who lives in the present and subjectively responds to current perceptions, relationships, and encounters. They disagree with the dark, pessimistic outlook of those in the Freudian psychoanalysis ranks, but rather view humanistic theories as positive and optimistic proposals which stress the tendency of the human personality toward growth and self-actualization. This progressing self will remain the center of its constantly changing world; worlds that will help mold the self but not necessarily confine it. Rather, the self has opportunity for maturation based on its encounters with this world. This understanding attempts to reduce the acceptance of hopeless redundancy. Humanistic therapy typically relies on the client for information of the past and its effect on the present, therefore the client dictates the type of guidance the therapist may initiate. This allows for an individualized approach to therapy. Rogers found patients differ in how they respond to other people. Rogers tried to model a particular approach to therapy- he stressed the reflective or empathetic response. This response type takes the client's viewpoint and reflects back his or her feeling and the context for it. An example of a reflective response would be, "It seems you are feeling anxious about your upcoming marriage". This response type seeks to clarify the therapist's understanding while also encouraging the client to think more deeply and seek to fully understand the feelings they have expressed.

Biopsychological Theories

Some of the earliest thinking about possible biological bases of personality grew out of the case of Phineas Gage. In an 1848 accident, a large iron rod was driven through Gage's head, and his personality apparently changed as a result (although descriptions of these psychological changes are usually exaggerated. (see the article on Gage). Graphic by Damasio *et al.* showing how the tamping iron may have damaged both frontal lobes. (A 2004 study by Ratiu and colleagues suggests the damage was more limited.)

In general, patients with brain damage have been difficult to find and study. In the 1990s, researchers began to use Electroencephalography (EEG), Positron Emission Tomography (PET) and more recently functional Magnetic Resonance Imaging (fMRI), which is now the most widely used imaging technique to help localize personality traits in the brain. One of the founders of this area of brain research is Richard Davidson of the University of Wisconsin–Madison. Davidson's research lab has focused on the role of the prefrontal cortex (PFC) and amygdala in manifesting human personality. In particular, this research has looked at hemispheric asymmetry of activity in these regions. Neuropsychological experiments have suggested that hemispheric asymmetry can affect an individual's personality (particularly in social settings) for individuals with NLD (non-verbal learning disorder), which is marked by the impairment of nonverbal information controlled by the right hemisphere of the brain. Progress will arise in the areas of gross motor skills, inability to organize visual-spatial relations, or adapt to novel social situations. Frequently, a person with NLD is unable to interpret non-verbal cues, and therefore experiences difficulty interacting with peers in socially normative ways.

One integrative, biopsychosocial approach to personality and psychopathology, linking brain and environmental factors to specific types of activity, is the hypostatic model of personality, created by Codrin Stefan Tapu.

SWOT analysis

SWOT analysis is a strategic planning method used to evaluate the Strengths, Weaknesses, Opportunities, and Threats involved in a project or in a business venture. It involves specifying the objective of the business venture or project and identifying the internal and external factors that are favorable and unfavorable to achieving that objective. The technique is credited to Albert Humphrey, who led a convention at Stanford University in the 1960s and 1970s using data from Fortune 500 companies.

A SWOT analysis must first start with defining a desired end state or objective. A SWOT analysis may be incorporated into the strategic planning model. Strategic Planning, including SWOT and SCAN analysis, has been the subject of much research.

- *Strengths:* attributes of the person or company that is helpful to achieving the objective(s).
- *Weaknesses:* attributes of the person or company that is harmful to achieving the objective(s).
- *Opportunities: external* conditions that is helpful to achieving the objective(s).
- *Threats: external* conditions which could do damage to the objective(s).

Identification of SWOTs is essential because subsequent steps in the process of planning for achievement of the selected objective may be derived from the SWOTs. First, the decision makers have to determine whether the objective is attainable, given the SWOTs. If the objective is NOT attainable a different objective must be selected and the process repeated. The SWOT analysis is often used in academia to highlight and identify strengths, weaknesses, opportunities and threats. It is particularly helpful in identifying areas for development.

Matching and Converting

Another way of utilizing SWOT is *matching* and *converting*.

Matching is used to find *competitive advantages* by matching the strengths to opportunities.

Converting is to apply conversion strategies to convert weaknesses or threats into strengths or opportunities. An example of conversion strategy is to find new markets. If the threats or weaknesses cannot be converted a company should try to *minimize* or *avoid* them.

Evidence on the Use of SWOT

SWOT analysis may limit the strategies considered in the evaluation. J. Scott Armstrong notes that "people who use SWOT might conclude that they have done an adequate job of planning and ignore such sensible things as defining the firm's objectives or calculating ROI for alternate strategies." Findings from Menon et al. (1999) and Hill and Westbrook (1997) have shown that SWOT may harm performance. As an alternative to SWOT, Armstrong describes a 5-step approach alternative that leads to better corporate performance. These criticisms are addressed to an old version of SWOT analysis that precedes the SWOT analysis described above under the heading "Strategic and Creative Use of SWOT Analysis." This old version did not require that SWOTs be derived from an agreed upon objective. Examples of SWOT analyses that do not state an objective are provided below under "Human Resources" and "Marketing."

Internal and External Factors

The aim of any SWOT analysis is to identify the key internal and external factors that are important to achieving the objective. These come from within the company's unique value chain. SWOT analysis groups key pieces of information into two main categories:

- *Internal factors:* The *strengths* and *weaknesses* internal to the organization.
- *External factors:* The *opportunities* and *threats* presented by the external environment to the organization. Use a PEST or PESTLE analysis to help identify factors.

The internal factors may be viewed as strengths or weaknesses depending upon their impact on the organization's objectives. What may represent strengths with respect to one objective may be weaknesses for another objective. The factors may include all of the 4P's; as well as personnel, finance, manufacturing capabilities, and so on. The external factors may include macroeconomic matters, technological change, legislation, and socio-cultural changes, as well as changes in the marketplace or competitive position. The results are often presented in the form of a matrix.

SWOT analysis is just one method of categorization and has its own weaknesses. For example, it may tend to persuade companies to compile lists rather than think about what is actually important in achieving objectives. It also presents the resulting lists uncritically and without clear prioritization so that, for example, weak opportunities may appear to balance strong threats. It is prudent not to eliminate too quickly any candidate SWOT entry. The importance of individual SWOTs will be revealed by the value of the strategies it generates. A SWOT item that produces valuable strategies is important. A SWOT item that generates no strategies is not important.

Use of SWOT Analysis

The usefulness of SWOT analysis is not limited to profit-seeking organizations. SWOT analysis may be used in any decision-making situation when a desired end-state (objective) has been defined. Examples include: non-profit organizations, governmental units, and individuals. SWOT analysis may also be used in pre-crisis planning and preventive crisis management. SWOT analysis may also be used in creating a recommendation during a viability study.

Self-esteem

Self-esteem is a term used in psychology to reflect a person's overall evaluation or appraisal of his or her own worth. Self-esteem encompasses beliefs (for example, "I am competent" or "I am incompetent") and emotions such as triumph, despair, pride and shame. A person's self-esteem may be reflected in their behaviour, such as in assertiveness, shyness, confidence or caution. Self-esteem can apply specifically to a particular dimension (for example, "I believe I am a good writer, and feel proud of that in particular") or have global extent (for example, "I believe I am a good person, and feel proud of myself in general").

Psychologists usually regard self-esteem as an enduring personality characteristic ("trait" self-esteem), though normal, short-term variations ("state" self-esteem) also exist. Synonyms or near-synonyms of self-esteem include: self-worth, self-regard, self-respect, self-love (which can express overtones of self-promotion), and self-integrity. Self-esteem is distinct from self-confidence and self-efficacy, which involve beliefs about ability and future performance.

Definitions

Given its long and varied history, the term has had no less than three major types of definition, each of which has generated its own tradition of research, findings, and practical applications:

1. The original definition presents self-esteem as a ratio found by dividing one's successes in areas of life of importance to a given individual by the failures in

them or one's "success/pretensions". Problems with this approach come from making self-esteem contingent upon success: this implies inherent instability because failure can occur at any moment.

2. In the mid 1960s Morris Rosenberg and social-learning theorists defined self-esteem in terms of a stable sense of personal worth or worthiness, (see Rosenberg self esteem scale). This became the most frequently used definition for research, but involves problems of boundary-definition, making self-esteem indistinguishable from such things as narcissism or simple bragging.
3. Nathaniel Branden in 1969 briefly defined self-esteem as "...the experience of being competent to cope with the basic challenges of life and being worthy of happiness". This two-factor approach, as some have also called it, provides a balanced definition that seems to be capable of dealing with limits of defining self-esteem primarily in terms of competence or worth alone.

Branden's (1969) description of self-esteem includes the following primary properties:

1. self-esteem as a basic human need, *i.e.,* "...it makes an essential contribution to the life process", "...is indispensable to normal and healthy self-development, and has a value for survival."
2. self-esteem as an automatic and inevitable consequence of the sum of individuals' choices in using their consciousness
3. something experienced as a part of, or background to, all of the individuals thoughts, feelings and actions.

Self esteem is a concept of personality, for it to grow, we need to have self worth, and this self worth will be sought from embracing challenges that result in the showing of success.

Compare the Usage of Terms Such as Self-love or Self-confidence.

Implicit self-esteem refers to a person's disposition to evaluate them selves positively or negatively in a spontaneous, automatic, or unconscious manner. It contrasts with *explicit self-esteem,* which entails more conscious and reflective self-evaluation. Both explicit self-esteem and implicit self-esteem are subtypes of self-esteem proper.

Implicit self-esteem is assessed using indirect measures of cognitive processing. These include the Name Letter Task and the Implicit Association Test. Such indirect measures are designed to reduce awareness of, or control of, the process of assessment. When used to assess implicit self-esteem, they feature stimuli designed to represent the self, such as personal pronouns (e.g., "I") or letters in one's name.

Measurement

For the purposes of empirical research, psychologists typically assess self-esteem by a self-report inventory yielding a quantitative result. They establish the validity and reliability of the questionnaire prior to its use. Researchers are becoming more interested in measures of implicit self-esteem.

Whereas popular lore recognizes just "high" self-esteem and "low" self-esteem, the Rosenberg Self-Esteem Scale (1965) and the Coopersmith Self-Esteem Inventory (1967/1981) both quantify it in more detail, and feature among the most widely used systems for measuring self-esteem. The Rosenberg test usually uses a ten-question battery scored on a four-point response system that requires participants to indicate their level of agreement with a series of statements about themselves. The Coopersmith Inventory uses a 50-question battery over a variety of topics and asks subjects whether they rate someone as similar or dissimilar to themselves.

Theories

Many early theories suggested that self-esteem is a basic human need or motivation. American psychologist Abraham Maslow, for example, included self-esteem in his hierarchy of needs. He described two different forms of esteem: the need for respect from others and the need for self-respect, or inner self-esteem. Respect from others entails recognition, acceptance, status, and appreciation, and was believed to be more fragile and easily lost than inner self-esteem. According to Maslow, without the fulfillment of the self-esteem need, individuals will be driven to seek it and unable to grow and obtain self-actualization. Modern theories of self-esteem explore the reasons why humans are motivated to maintain a high regard for them selves. Sociometer theory maintains that self-esteem evolved to check one's level of status and acceptance in ones' social group. According to terror management theory, self-esteem serves a protective function and reduces anxiety about life and death.

Self-knowledge

Self-knowledge is a term used in psychology to describe the information that an individual draws upon when finding an answer to the question *"what am I like?"*.

Self-knowledge is a prerequisite of self-consciousness (not to be confused with consciousness as a raw subject) alongside self-awareness. However, self-awareness may in itself be a necessary condition for self-knowledge to be sought after and developed in the first place. Self-awareness alone is not enough for a being to be considered self-conscious; young infants and even animals display elements of simple self-awareness and agency/contingency. However it requires a greater level of cognition for a creature to become truly self-conscious. It is the knowledge of one's self and one's properties and the *desire* to seek such knowledge that guide the development of the self concept. Self-knowledge informs us of our mental representations of ourselves, which contain attributes that we uniquely pair with ourselves, and theories on whether these attributes are stable, or dynamic.

Self-knowledge is a component of the self, or more accurately, the *self-concept.* The self-concept is thought to have three primary aspects:

- The Cognitive Self
- The Affective Self
- The Executive Self

Self-knowledge is linked to the *cognitive self* in that its motives guide our search to gain greater clarity and assurance that our own self-concept is an accurate representation of our *true self*; for this reason the cognitive self is also referred to as the *known self*. The cognitive self is made up of everything we know (or *think we know* about ourselves). This implies physiological properties such as hair color, race, and height etc.; and psychological properties like beliefs, values, and dislikes to name but a few. The affective and executive selves are also known as the *felt* and *active* selves respectively, as they refer to the emotional and behavioral components of the self-concept.

Communication Skills—Start Here!

Why you need to get your message across

Effective communication is all about conveying your messages to other people clearly and unambiguously. It's also about receiving information that others are sending to you, with as little distortion as possible. Doing this involves effort from both the sender of the message and the receiver. And it's a process that can be fraught with error, with messages muddled by the sender, or misinterpreted by the recipient. When this isn't detected, it can cause tremendous confusion, wasted effort and missed opportunity.

In fact, communication is only successful when both the sender and the receiver understand the same information as a result of the communication. By successfully getting your message across, you convey your thoughts and ideas effectively. When not successful, the thoughts and ideas that you actually send do not necessarily reflect what you think, causing a communications breakdown and creating roadblocks that stand in the way of your goals - both personally and professionally.

In a recent survey of recruiters from companies with more than 50,000 employees, communication skills were cited as the single more important decisive factor in choosing managers. The survey, conducted by the University of Pittsburgh's Katz Business School, points out that communication skills, including written and oral presentations, as well as an ability to work with others, are the main factor contributing to job success. In spite of the increasing importance placed on communication skills, many individuals continue to struggle, unable to communicate their thoughts and ideas effectively - whether in verbal or written format. This inability makes it nearly impossible for them to compete effectively in the workplace, and stands in the way of career progression.

Being able to communicate effectively is therefore essential if you want to build a successful career. To do this, you must understand what your message is, what audience you are sending it to, and how it will be perceived. You must also weigh-in the circumstances surrounding your communications, such as situational and cultural context.

Communications Skills—The Importance of Removing Barriers

Problems with communication can pop-up at every stage of the communication process (which consists of the *sender*, *encoding*, the *channel*, *decoding*, the *receiver*, *feedback* and the *context* - see the diagram below). At each stage, there is the potential for misunderstanding and confusion.

The Communications Process

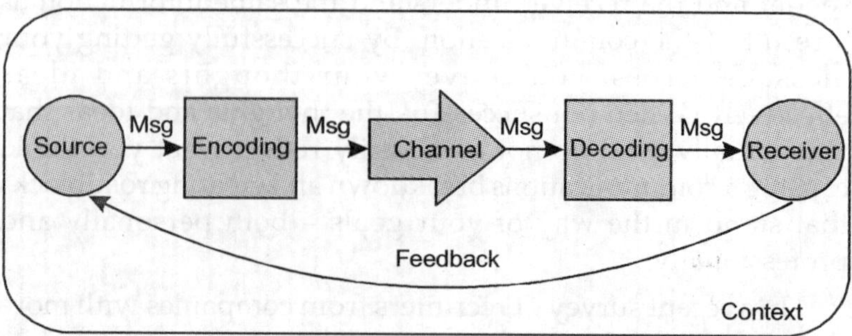

To be an effective communicator and to get your point across without misunderstanding and confusion, your goal should be to lessen the frequency of problems at each stage of this process, with clear, concise, accurate, well-planned communications. We follow the process through below:

Source

As the source of the message, you need to be clear about why you're communicating, and what you want to communicate. You also need to be confident that the information you're communicating is useful and accurate.

Message

The message is the information that you want to communicate.

Encoding

This is the process of transferring the information you want to communicate into a form that can be sent and correctly decoded at the other end. Your success in encoding depends partly on your ability to convey information clearly and simply, but also on your ability to anticipate and eliminate sources of confusion (for example, cultural issues, mistaken assumptions, and missing information.) A key part of this knows your audience: Failure to understand who you are communicating with will result in delivering messages that are misunderstood.

Channel

Messages are conveyed through channels, with verbal channels including face-to-face meetings, telephone and videoconferencing; and written channels including letters, emails, memos and reports. Different channels have different strengths and weaknesses. For example, it's not particularly effective to give a long list of directions verbally, while you'll quickly cause problems if you give someone negative feedback using email.

Decoding

Just as successful encoding is a skill, so is successful decoding (involving, for example, taking the time to read a message carefully, or listen actively to it.) Just as confusion can arise from errors in encoding, it can also arise from decoding errors. This is particularly the case if the decoder doesn't have enough knowledge to understand the message.

Receiver

Your message is delivered to individual members of your audience. No doubt, you have in mind the actions or reactions you hope your message will get from this audience. Keep in mind, though, that each of these individuals enters into the communication process with ideas and feelings that will undoubtedly influence their understanding of your message, and their response. To be a successful communicator, you should consider these before delivering your message, and act appropriately.

Feedback

Your audience will provide you with feedback, as verbal and nonverbal reactions to your communicated message. Pay close attention to this feedback, as it is the only thing that can give you confidence that your audience has understood your message. If you find that there has been a misunderstanding, at least you have the opportunity to send the message a second time.

Context

The situation in which your message is delivered is the context. This may include the surrounding environment or broader culture (corporate culture, international cultures, and so on).

Removing Barriers at All These Stages

To deliver your messages effectively, you must commit to breaking down the barriers that exist within each of these stages of the communication process. Let's begin with the message itself. If your message is too lengthy, disorganized, or contains errors, you can expect the message to be misunderstood and misinterpreted. Use of poor verbal and body language can also confuse the message. Barriers in context tend to stem from senders offering too much information too fast. When in doubt here, less is oftentimes more. It is best to be mindful of the demands on other people's time, especially in today's ultra-busy society.

Once you understand this, you need to work to understand your audience's culture, making sure you can converse and deliver your message to people of different backgrounds and cultures within your own organization, in your country and even abroad. The first skill that you'll learn in this communications skills section of MindTools.com is 'How to Make a Great First Impression": This is essential if you're going to have the chance to communicate your message. To read this, click 'Next article' below.

How to Communicate: Improve Your Relationships with Effective Communication Skills

Conflict in a relationship is virtually inevitable. In itself, conflict isn't a problem; how it's handled, however, can bring people together or tear them apart. Poor communication skills, disagreements and misunderstandings can be a source of anger and distance, or a springboard to a stronger relationship and happier future. Next time you're dealing with conflict, keep these tips on effective communication skills in mind and you can create a more positive outcome.

1. ***Stay Focused:*** Sometimes it's tempting to bring up past seemingly related conflicts when dealing with current ones. Unfortunately, this often clouds the issue and makes finding mutual understanding and a solution to *the current issue* less likely, and makes the whole discussion more taxing and even confusing. Try not to bring up past hurts or other topics. Stay focused on the present, your feelings, understanding one another and finding a solution.

2. ***Listen Carefully:*** People often *think* they're listening, but are really thinking about what they're going to say next when the other person stops talking. Truly effective communication goes both ways. While it might be difficult, try really listening to what your partner is saying. Don't interrupt. Don't get defensive. Just hear them and reflect back what they're saying so they know you've heard. Then you'll understand them better and they'll be more willing to listen to you.

3. ***Try To See Their Point of View:*** In a conflict, most of us primarily want to feel heard and understood. We talk a lot about our point of view to get the other person to see things our way. Ironically, if we all do this all the time, there's little focus on the other person's point of view, and nobody feels understood. Try to really see the other side, and then you can better explain yours. (If you don't 'get it', ask more questions until you do.) Others will more likely be willing to listen if they feel heard.

4. ***Respond to Criticism with Empathy:*** When someone comes at you with criticism, it's easy to feel that they're wrong, and get defensive. While criticism is hard to hear, and often exaggerated or colored by the other person's emotions, it's important to listen for the other person's pain and respond with empathy for their feelings. Also, look for what's true in what they're saying; that can be valuable information for you.

5. Own What's Yours: Realize that personal responsibility is strength, not a weakness. Effective communication involves admitting when you're wrong. If you share some responsibility in a conflict (which is usually the case), look for and admit to what's yours. It diffuses the situation, sets a good example, and shows maturity. It also often inspires the other person to respond in kind, leading you both closer to mutual understanding and a solution.

6. Use "I" Messages: Rather than saying things like, "*You* really messed up here," begin statements with "I", and make them about yourself and your feelings, like, "I feel frustrated when this happens." It's less accusatory, sparks less defensiveness, and helps the other person understand your point of view rather than feeling attacked.

7. Look for Compromise: Instead of trying to 'win' the argument, look for solutions that meet everybody's needs. Either through compromise or a new solution that gives you both what you want most, this focus is much more effective than one person getting what they want at the other's expense. Healthy communication involves finding a resolution that both sides can be happy with.

8. Take a Time-Out: Sometimes tempers get heated and it's just too difficult to continue a discussion without it becoming an argument or a fight. If you feel yourself or your partner starting to get too angry to be constructive or showing some destructive communication patterns, its okay to take a break from the discussion until you both cool off. Sometimes good communication means knowing when to take a break.

9. Don't Give Up: While taking a break from the discussion is sometimes a good idea, always come back to it. If you both approach the situation with a constructive attitude, mutual respect, and a willingness to see the other's point of view or at least find a solution, you can make progress toward the goal of a resolution to the conflict. Unless it's time to give up on the relationship, don't give up on communication.

10. Ask For Help If You Need It: If one or both of you has trouble staying respectful during conflict, or if you've tried resolving conflict with your partner on your own and the situation just doesn't seem to be improving, you might benefit from a few sessions with a therapist. Couples counseling or family therapy can provide help with altercations and teach skills to resolve future conflict. If your partner doesn't want to go, you can still often benefit from going alone.

Interpersonal Relationship

An *interpersonal relationship* is an association between two or more people that may range from fleeting to enduring. This association may be based on limerence, love and liking, regular business interactions, or some other type of social commitment. Interpersonal relationships take place in a great variety of contexts, such as family, friends, marriage, associates, work, clubs, neighborhoods, and churches. They may be regulated by law, custom, or mutual agreement, and are the basis of social groups and society as a whole. Although humans are fundamentally social creatures, interpersonal relationships are not always healthy. Examples of unhealthy relationships include abusive relationships and codependence.

A relationship is normally viewed as a connection between two individuals, such as a romantic or intimate relationship, or a parent-child relationship. Individuals can also have relationships with groups of people, such as the relation between a pastor and his congregation, an uncle and a family, or a mayor and a town. Finally, groups or even nations may have relations with each other, though this is a much broader domain than that covered under the topic of interpersonal relationships. See such articles as international relations for more information on associations between groups. Most scholarly work on relationships focuses on romantic partners in pairs or dyads. These intimate relationships are, however, only a small subset of interpersonal relationships. Interpersonal relationships also can include friendships, such as relationships involving individuals providing relational care to marginalized persons. These relationships usually involve some level of interdependence. People in a relationship tend to influence each other, share their thoughts and feelings, and engage in activities together. Because of this interdependence, most things that change or impact one member of the relationship will have some level of impact on the other member. The study of interpersonal relationships involves several branches of the social sciences, including such disciplines as sociology, psychology, anthropology, and social work.

Types

Close relationships are important for emotional wellbeing throughout the lifespan. Interpersonal relationships include kinship and family relations in which people become associated by genetics or consanguinity. These include such roles as father, mother, son, or daughter. Relationships can also be established by marriage, such as husband, wife, father-in-law, mother-in-law, uncle by marriage, or aunt by marriage. They may be formal long-term relationships recognized by law and formalized through public ceremony, such as marriage or civil union. They may also be informal long-term relationships such as loving relationships or romantic relationships with or without living together. In these cases the "other person" is often called lover, boyfriend, or girlfriend, as distinct from just a male or female friend, or "significant other". If the partners live together, the relationship may resemble marriage, with the parties possibly even called husband and wife. Scottish common law can regard such couples as actual marriages after a period of time. Long-term relationships in other countries can become known as common-law marriages, although they may have no special status in law. The term *mistress* may refer in a somewhat old-fashioned way to a female lover of an already married or unmarried man. A mistress may have the status of an "official mistress" (in French *maîtresse en titre*); as exemplified by the career of Madame de Pompadour.

The status of a relationship goes along with the way we communicate with them. Interpersonal relationships and communication is a two-way street, which needs to be clear by both ends. The way we communicate with our significant other is not the same as we communicate of our bosses or little brother. The transmission model of communication has five main parts according to Karen Reynolds essay: Information Source-where the message is produced Transmitter-where the message is encoded Channel-where the signal is carried Receiver- where the message is decoded Destination-where the message ends up However, noise can interfere with the channel and change the original message. This can relate to interpersonal relationships because the sender and receiver of messages need to be on the same of page of the context of the message so the message will not be taken the wrong way according to the Karen Reynolds. If the message is taken the wrong way, it could be detrimental to the relationship. Communication is a very important component to a successful relationship. As time goes on people's attitudes change because they have become more comfortable with a person. This could hurt the way the sender may send the message or the receiver interprets the message. In Daniel Chandler's essay, he states that no allowance is made for unequal power relations. In other words, he is saying that individuals will not always feel that the other person's ideas are valuable or creditable. In an interpersonal relationship point of view, a man could never believe what the girlfriend is saying according to his own standards, which would cause havoc in their communication. The way to interpret a person who communicates is different depending on the person; therefore, the transmission model is a hard way to partake in an interpersonal relationship, because the interpretation of a message can change at any time.

Friendships consist of mutual liking, trust, respect, and often even love and unconditional acceptance. They usually imply the discovery or establishment of similarities or common ground between the individuals. Internet friendships and pen-pals may take place at a considerable physical distance. Brotherhood and sisterhood can refer to individuals united in a common cause or having a common interest, which may involve formal membership in a club, organization, association, society, lodge, fraternity, or sorority. This type of interpersonal relationship relates to the comradeship of fellow soldiers in peace or war. Partners or co-workers in a profession, business, or common workplace also have a long term interpersonal relationship.

Soulmates are individuals intimately drawn to one another through a favorable meeting of minds and who find mutual acceptance and understanding with one another. Soulmates may feel themselves bonded together for a lifetime and hence may become sexual partners, but not necessarily. Casual relationships are sexual relationships extending beyond one-night stands that exclusively consist of sexual behavior. One can label the participants as "friends with benefits" or as friends "hooking up" when limited to sexual intercourse, or regard them as sexual partners in a wider sense. Platonic love is an affectionate relationship into which the sexual element does not enter, especially in cases where one might easily assume otherwise.

Development

Interpersonal relationships are dynamic systems that change continuously during their existence. Like living organisms, relationships have a beginning, a lifespan, and an end. They tend to grow and improve gradually, as people get to know each other and become closer emotionally, or they gradually deteriorate as people drift apart, move on with their lives and form new relationships with others. One of the most influential models of relationship development was proposed by psychologist George Levinger. This model was formulated to describe heterosexual, adult romantic relationships, but it has been applied to other kinds of interpersonal relations as well. According to the model, the natural development of a relationship follows five stages:

1. ***Acquaintance:*** Becoming acquainted depends on previous relationships, physical proximity, first impressions, and a variety of other factors. If two people begin to like each other, continued interactions may lead to the next stage, but acquaintance can continue indefinitely.
2. ***Buildup:*** During this stage, people begin to trust and care about each other. The need for compatibility and such filtering agents as common background and goals will influence whether or not interaction continues.
3. ***Continuation:*** This stage follows a mutual commitment to a long term friendship, romantic relationship, or marriage. It is generally a long, relative stable period. Nevertheless, continued growth and development will occur during this time. Mutual trust is important for sustaining the relationship.
4. ***Deterioration:*** Not all relationships deteriorate, but those that do, tend to show signs of trouble. Boredom, resentment, and dissatisfaction may occur, and individuals may communicate less and avoid self-disclosure. Loss of trust and betrayals may take place as the downward spiral continues.
5. ***Termination:*** The final stage marks the end of the relationship, either by death in the case of a healthy relationship, or by separation.

Friendships may involve some degree of transitivity. In other words, a person may become a friend of an existing friend's friend. However, if two people have a sexual relationship with the same person, they may become competitors rather than friends. Accordingly, sexual behavior with the sexual partner of a friend may damage the friendship (see love triangle). Sexual relations between two friends tend to alter that relationship, either by "taking it to the next level" or by severing it. Sexual partners may also be classified as friends and the sexual relationship may either enhance or depreciate the friendship.

Legal sanction reinforces and regularizes marriages and civil unions as perceived "respectable" building-blocks of society. In the United States of America, for example, the decriminalization of homosexual sexual relations in the Supreme Court decision, Lawrence v. Texas (2003) facilitated the mainstreaming of gay long-term relationships, and broached the possibility of the legalization of same-sex marriages in that country.

Soft Skills

Soft skills is a sociological term relating to a person's "EQ" (Emotional Intelligence Quotient), the cluster of personality traits, social graces, communication, language, personal habits, friendliness, and optimism that characterize relationships with other people. Soft skills complement hard skills (part of a person's IQ), which are the occupational requirements of a job and many other activities.

A person's soft skill EQ is an important part of their individual contribution to the success of an organization. Particularly those organizations dealing with customers face-to-face are generally more successful if they train their staff to use these skills. Screening or training for personal habits or traits such as dependability and conscientiousness can yield significant return on investment for an organization. For this reason, soft skills are increasingly sought out by employers in addition to standard qualifications. It has been suggested that in a number of professions soft skills may be more important over the long term than occupational skills. The legal profession is one example where the ability to deal with people effectively and politely, more than their mere occupational skills, can determine the professional success of a lawyer.

Examples of Soft Skills

- Participate in a team (see team building)
- Lead a team (see leadership)
- Unite a team amidst cultural differences
- Teach others
- Coach others
- Motivate others
- Provide services
- Negotiate
- Decision making
- Problem solving
- Observe forms of etiquette
- Active Listening
- Maintain meaningless conversation (small talk)
- Maintain meaningful conversation (discussion/debate)
- Defuse arguments with timing, instructions and polite, concise language
- Foresee situations

Top 60 Soft Skills

The Workforce Profile defined about 60 "soft skills", which employers seek. They are applicable to any field of work, according to the study, and are the "personal traits and skills that employers state are the most important when selecting employees for jobs of any type."

1. Math.
2. Safety.
3. Courtesy.
4. Honesty.
5. Grammar.

6. Reliability.
7. Flexibility.
8. Team skills.
9. Eye contact.
10. Cooperation.
11. Adaptability.
12. Follow rules.
13. Self-directed.
14. Good attitudes.
15. Writing skills.
16. Driver's license.
17. Dependability.
18. Advanced math.
19. Self-supervising.
20. Good references.
21. Being drug free.
22. Good attendance.
23. Personal energy.
24. Work experience.
25. Ability to measure.
26. Personal integrity.
27. Good work history.
28. Positive work ethic.
29. Interpersonal skills.
30. Motivational skills.
31. Valuing education.
32. Personal chemistry.
33. Willingness to learn.
34. Common sense.

35. Critical thinking skills.
36. Knowledge of fractions.
37. Reporting to work on time.
38. Use of rulers and calculators.
39. Good personal appearance.
40. Wanting to do a good job.
41. Basic spelling and grammar.
42. Reading and comprehension.
43. Ability to follow regulations.
44. Willingness to be accountable.
45. Ability to fill out a job application.
46. Ability to make production quotas.
47. Basic manufacturing skills training.
48. Awareness of how business works.
49. Staying on the job until it is finished.
50. Ability to read and follow instructions.
51. Willingness to work second and third shifts.
52. Caring about seeing the company succeed.
53. Understanding what the world is all about.
54. Ability to listen and document what you have heard.
55. Commitment to continued training and learning.
56. Willingness to take instruction and responsibility.
57. Ability to relate to coworkers in a close environment.
58. Not expecting to become a supervisor in the first six months.
59. Willingness to be a good worker and go beyond the traditional eight-hour day.
60. Communication skills with public, fellow employees, supervisors, and customers.

Common Fears of Public Speaking

What happens when you have to speak in public?

Did you know that public speaking tops the list of phobias for most people? Not spiders or heights—public speaking—speech in public! Well, if you didn't know that, we bet your body does. It will do all kinds of unpleasant things to you when you have to stand up and face a sea of faces with the hope of getting your message across in a compelling and interesting way. Your hands may sweat and your mouth goes dry. Your knees may shake and a quaver affects your voice. Your heart may race and those well known butterflies invade your stomach.

When all that happen most people don't think of getting their message across in a compelling and interesting way; they just think of getting off the 'stage' as quickly as possible! We don't really mean to frighten you, just remind you that your body reacts 'in extremis' when put under pressure, and for most people, public speaking is just about the worst pressure they can be put under. It's normal to be nervous and have a lot of anxiety when speaking in public. In a way, it's less normal not to have nerves or anxiety; in fact, to feel you have a phobia about public speaking.

Why do we get Public Speaking anxiety?

Fight or flight

Our bodies are geared to fight or flight from ancient time—fight that mastodon or get the hell out of the way. We don't have too many mastodons around these days, but the body still reacts as though we do. So, if we have to get up and speak in public, all that adrenalin and noradrenalin goes coursing through our bodies—way more than we need. We can't run away (well, we could, but we'd be out of job pretty quick if we did it too often), so our only option is to fight. But in terms of speaking in public, it can be hard to define just what we're fighting.

Why does public speaking do this to us?

Good question. You'd think that for most people, being given the opportunity to impress their audience would be a fantastic one. There you are in front of a group of people, the spotlight is on you and for the length of time you've been giving and the world is yours. The very fact that the spotlight is you is enough to trigger every fear, anxiety and phobia you've ever had about public speaking.

Here's why

- You may be judged by all those people, and judged badly
- You may feel like a fool
- You might make mistakes and lose your way
- You'll be completely humiliated
- You'll never be as good as ________ (fill in the blank)
- 'They' won't like you
- 'They' won't 'get' what you're trying to say

How to Overcome Fear of Public Speaking

What good are Nerves

Public speaking may not be comfortable, but take our word for it, nerves are good. Being 'centre stage' is not a good place to feel too comfortable. Nerves will keep you awake and ensure you don't get too complacent. Hard to feel complacent when your heart is beating so hard you're sure everyone watching you can hear it.If channelled well, nerves can make the difference between giving a humdrum presentation and giving one that keeps people listening.

Get your Attention off Yourself

It's very tempting to keep focused on how you're feeling, especially if you're feeling really uncomfortable. You'll start to notice every bead of sweat. To make your nerves work for you, you need to focus on just about anything other than yourself. You can distract yourself by paying attention to the environment in which you're speaking and seeing how you can make it work for you.

Once you're actually in front of your audience, pay attention to them. If you can, notice how people are dressed, who's wearing glasses, which has on bright colours. There will be dozens and dozens of things you can pay attention to help you trick your mind into not noticing what's going on with you. Anything will do and you will find that the less you concentrate on how you are feeling and the more you concentrate on other things, the more confident you will feel.

Your audience can be your friend

Unless you know you're absolutely facing a hostile group of people, human nature is such that your audience wants you succeed. They're on your side! Therefore, rather than assuming they don't like you; give them the benefit of the doubt that they do. They aren't an anonymous sea of faces, but real people. So to help you gain more confidence when speaking in public, think of ways to engage your audience. Remember, even if they aren't speaking, you can still have a two-way conversation. When you make an important point pay attention to the people who are nodding in agreement and the ones who are frowning in disagreement. As long as you are creating a reaction in your audience you are in charge.

Keep them awake

The one thing you don't want is for them to fall asleep! But make no mistake public speaking arenas are designed to do just that: dim lights, cushy chairs, not having to open their mouths—a perfect invitation to catch up on those zzzzs.

Ways to keep them awake include

- Ask rhetorical questions
- Maintain eye contact for a second or two with as many people as possible

- Be provocative
- Be challenging
- Change the pace of your delivery
- Change the volume of your voice

Public Speaking Training

Get a coach

Whatever the presentation public speaking is tough, so get help. Since there are about a zillion companies out there all ready to offer you public speaking training and courses, here are some things to look for when deciding the training that's right for you.

Focus on positives not negatives

Any training you do to become more effective at public speaking should always focus on the positive aspects of what you already do well. Nothing can undermine confidence more than telling someone what they aren't doing well. You already do lots of things well good public speaking training should develop those instead of telling you what you shouldn't do.

Turn your back on too many rules

If you find a public speaking course that looks as though it's going to give you lots of dos and don'ts, walk away! Your brain is going to be so full of whatever it is you're going to be talking about that to try to cram it full of a whole bunch of rules will just be counterproductive. As far as we're concerned, aside from physical violence or inappropriately taking off your clothes, there are no hard and fast rules about public speaking.

You are an individual not a clone

Most importantly, good public speaking training should treat you as a unique individual, with your own quirks and idiosyncrasies. You aren't like anybody else and your training course should help you bring out your individuality, not try to turn you into someone you're not.

Hints and Tips for Effective Public Speaking

Here are just a few hints, public speaking tips and techniques to help you develop your skills and become far more effective as a public speaker.

Mistakes

Mistakes are all right. Recovering from mistakes makes you appear more human.

Good recovery puts your audience at ease—they identify with you more.

Humour

Tell jokes if you're good at telling joke. If you aren't good, best to leave the jokes behind. There's nothing worse than a punch line that has no punch. Gentle humor is good in place of jokes. Self-deprecation is good, but tries not to lay it on too thick.

Tell stories

Stories make you a real person not just a deliverer of information. Use personal experiences to bring your material to life. No matter how dry your material is, you can always find a way to humanise it.

How to use the public speaking environment

Try not to get stuck in one place. Use all the space that's available to you. Move around. One way to do this is to leave your notes in one place and move to another. If your space is confined (say a meeting room or even presenting at a table) use stronger body language to convey your message.

Technology

Speak to your audience not your slides. Your slides are there to support you not the other way around. Ideally, slides should be graphics and not words (people read faster than they hear and will be impatient for you to get to the next point).If all the technology on offer fails; it's still you they've come to hear.

The 25 Public Speaking Skills Every Speaker Must Have

Inspired by 25 Skills Every Man Should Know, I pondered a list of the *25 essential skills every public speaker should have.* How did I do? Every public speaker should be able to:

1. ***Research a topic:*** Good speakers stick to what they know. Great speakers research what they need to convey their message.
2. ***Focus:*** Help your audience grasp your message by focusing on your message. Stories, humour, or other "sidebars" should connect to the core idea. Anything that doesn't needs to be edited out.
3. ***Organize ideas logically:*** A well-organized presentation can be absorbed with minimal mental strain. Bridging is key.
4. ***Employ quotations, facts, and statistics:*** Don't include these for the sake of including them, but do use them appropriately to complement your ideas.
5. ***Master metaphors:*** Metaphors enhance the understandability of the message in a way that direct language often can not.
6. ***Tell a story:*** Everyone loves a story. Points wrapped up in a story are more memorable, too!
7. ***Start strong and close stronger:*** The body of your presentation should be strong too, but your audience

will remember your first and last words (if, indeed, they remember anything at all).

8. ***Incorporate humour:*** Knowing when to use humour is essential. So is developing the comedic timing to deliver it with greatest effect.
9. ***Vary vocal pace, tone, and volume:*** A monotone voice is like fingernails on the chalkboard.
10. ***Punctuate words with gestures:*** Gestures should complement your words in harmony. Tell them how big the fish was, and show them with your arms.
11. ***Utilize 3-dimensional space:*** Chaining yourself to the lectern limits the energy and passion you can exhibit. Lose the notes, and lose the chain.
12. ***Complement words with visual aids:*** Visual aids should *aid* the message; they should not *be* the message. Read *slide: logy* or the *Presentation Zen* book and adopt the techniques.
13. ***Analyze the audience:*** Deliver the message they want (or need) to hear.
14. ***Connect with the audience:*** Eye contact is only the first step. Aim to have the audience conclude "This speaker is just like me!" The sooner, the better.
15. ***Interact with the audience:*** Ask questions (and care about the answers). Solicit volunteers. Make your presentation a dialogue.
16. ***Conduct a Q&A session:*** Not every speaking opportunity affords a Q&A session, but understands how to lead one productively. Use the Q&A to solidify the impression that you are an expert, not (just) a speaker.
17. ***Lead a discussion:*** Again, not every speaking opportunity affords time for a discussion, but know how to engage the audience productively.
18. ***Obey time constraints:*** Maybe you have 2 minutes. Maybe you have 45. Either way, customize your

presentation to fit the time allowed, and respect your audience by not going over time.

19. *Craft an introduction:* Set the context and make sure the audience is ready to go, whether the introduction is for you or for someone else.
20. *Exhibit confidence and poise:* These qualities are sometimes difficult for a speaker to attain, but easy for an audience to sense.
21. *Handle unexpected issues smoothly:* Maybe the lights will go out. Maybe the projector is dead. Have a plan to handle every situation.
22. *Be coherent when speaking off the cuff:* Impromptu speaking (before, after, or during a presentation) leaves a lasting impression too. Doing it well tells the audience that you are personable, and that you are an expert who knows their stuff beyond the slides and prepared speech.
23. *Seek and utilize feedback:* Understand that no presen-tation or presenter (yes, even you!) is perfect. Aim for continuous improvement, and understand that the best way to improve is to solicit candid feedback from as many people as you can.
24. *Listen critically and analyze other speakers:* Study the strengths and weakness of other speakers.
25. *Act and speak ethically:* Since public speaking fears are so common, realize the tremendous power of influence that you hold. Use this power responsibly.

How to Develop Good Public Speaking Skills

We all think about how to develop good public speaking skills at a professional level. People have different concepts in their mind and they always think that they will be overlooked by the audience in general. This is the reason why most of the people do not get themselves involved in the public speaking. Public speaking is a very broad term. Sometimes people get so confused and scared that their tongue gets tied and they meltdown in the public. This is just because of their internal fear. Though they know their topic in depth, because of the internal fear they just break down in public. Some people say that the art of public speaking comes through constant practice and some think that public speakers are born.

How to develop good public speaking skills is a big question for numerous people. There are people who develop public speaking skills in a few months of practice but for some it takes years to develop. But overall it is practice that counts. Some people who think that public speaking skills are not for them but they are for the people who are in marketing or sales. But people should understand that this is not true. No doubt a good public speaker should have good communication and interpersonal skills. But that too comes after years of practice.

Good public speaking skills also works at the time of the interview. It is compulsory to face an interview before getting a new job. Interviewer will not only judge your personality but also your communication and fluency in general. In this tech world not only your basic qualification is counted but your presentation skills and public speaking skills are also counted. It is not that we only require public speaking skills to speak in front of audience or to give lectures. Public speaking skills are an asset that is worth millions. Not only public speaking skills are counted in professional life but are also useful when a person is college go-getter.

For example a student possessing good presentation skills and public speaking skills can do wonders in his grading criteria. All that matters is clarity of delivery element, which is the base of any public speaking skills. It is important to have clarity of delivery element because unclear speech and words will do any good in general speaking in front of audiences. All the eyes are on you and all the ears are on your words. So, it is imperative to have clarity of delivery. It is common sense that on whatever topic you are speaking, clarity is a must because no one would be able to convey your message or whatever you are trying to speak. Unclear words will only show that you have not prepared the subject or you are scared of speaking. Those people who cannot convey their ideas into words cannot transform their skills in professional life. Some scholars have just passed away with their ideas still left with them just because of the inability to transform ideas. It is true that these scholars were intelligent and conveyed their message through writing. But we all know that written scripts cannot convey the messages effectively compared to speaking.

They simply were not able to put their messages in front of the people of what they actually think. They were unable to speak in front of the public. So, do not let go the importance of public speaking skills. People also think that public speaking skills and communication skills are not inter-related. But they should know that they are inter-related to a certain degree of extent. However public speaking is a broader term compared to communication skills because people with good public speaking skills have good communication skills. But this is not the case with the people possessing good communication skills, because people with good communication skills may or may not have good public speaking skills. There are many reasons behind why people with good communication cannot speak in public. The reason behind why people are unable to speak in front of pubic is fear. Most of the people are scared and have fear while speaking in front of the public. They get nervous and their heartbeat gets fast resulting into unclear words and stammering. There are numerous ways to enhance public speaking skills. No doubt apart from the practice you should have a great storage bank of vocabulary in your mind. You can practice public speaking skills speaking in front of your family members, friends and colleagues.

Perception

In philosophy, psychology, and cognitive science, *perception* is the process of attaining awareness or understanding of sensory information. The word "perception" comes from the Latin words *perception, percipient,* and means "receiving, collecting, action of taking possession, apprehension with the mind or senses." Perception is one of the oldest fields in psychology. The oldest quantitative law in psychology is the Weber-Fechner law, which quantifies the relationship between the intensity of physical stimuli and their perceptual effects. The study of perception gave rise to the Gestalt school of psychology, with its emphasis on holistic approach. What one perceives is a result of interplays between past experiences, including one's culture, and the interpretation of the perceived. If the percept does not have support in any of these perceptual bases it is unlikely to rise above perceptual threshold.

Types

Two types of consciousness are considerable regarding perception: phenomenal (any occurrence that is observable and physical) and psychological. The difference everybody can demonstrate to him- or herself is by the simple opening and closing of his or her eyes: phenomenal consciousness is thought, on average, to be predominately absent without sight. Through the full or rich sensations present in sight, nothing by comparison is present while the eyes are closed. Using this precept, it is understood that, in the vast majority of cases, logical solutions are reached through simple human sensation. The analogy of Plato's Cave was coined to express these ideas.

Passive perception (conceived by René Descartes) can be surmised as the following sequence of events: surrounding '! input (senses) '! processing (brain) '! output (re-action). Although still supported by mainstream philosophers, psychologists and neurologists, this theory is nowadays losing momentum. The theory of active perception has emerged from extensive research of sensory illusions, most notably the works of Richard L. Gregory. This theory, which is increasingly gaining experimental support, can be surmised as dynamic relationship between "description" (in the brain) "! senses "! surrounding, all of which holds true to the linear concept of experience.

Assertiveness

To be assertive is not, as some people imagine, to be overbearing and aggressive, but to be straightforward, open and honest. It means that you relate well to people, able to express your needs freely, take responsibility for your feelings and stand up for yourself when necessary. In conflict situations you seek, where possible, to reach a 'win-win' outcome, in which the needs of all parties are fully acknowledged. In order to appreciate the nature of assertiveness it may be useful to examine various forms of non-assertive behaviour. There are three primary types, as follows:

- *Aggressive behaviour:* This may occur where a person is trying to impose their views inappropriately on others, and it may be accompanied by threatening language and an angry, glaring expression.
- *Submissive behaviour:* This is the opposite of aggressive behaviour. Here the person acts like a doormat, downplaying their own needs and willing to fit in with the wishes of others in order to keep the peace at any price. It may be accompanied by general passivity, nervousness and a lack of eye contact.

Motivation is the activation or energization of goal-oriented behavior. Motivation is said to be intrinsic or extrinsic. The term is generally used for humans but, theoretically, it can also be used to describe the causes for animal behavior as well. This article refers to human motivation. According to various theories, motivation may be rooted in the basic need to minimize physical pain and maximize pleasure, or it may include specific needs such as eating and resting, or a desired object, hobby, goal, state of being, ideal, or it may be attributed to less-apparent reasons such as altruism, selfishness, morality, or avoiding mortality. Conceptually, motivation should not be confused with either volition or optimism.

Motivation Concepts

Intrinsic motivation comes from rewards inherent to a task or activity itself – the enjoyment of a puzzle or the love of playing. This form of motivation has been studied by social and educational psychologists since the early 1970s. Research has found that it is usually associated with high educational achievement and enjoyment by students. Intrinsic motivation has been explained by Fritz Heider's attribution theory, Bandura's work on self-efficacy, and Ryan and Deci's cognitive evaluation theory. Students are likely to be intrinsically motivated if they:

- attribute their educational results to internal factors that they can control (e.g. the amount of effort they put in),
- believe they can be effective agents in reaching desired goals (i.e. the results are not determined by luck),
- are interested in mastering a topic, rather than just rote-learning to achieve good grades.

Extrinsic Motivation

Extrinsic motivation comes from outside of the performer. Money is the most obvious example, but coercion and threat of punishment are also common extrinsic motivations. While competing, the crowd may cheer on the performer, which may motivate him or her to do well. Trophies are also extrinsic incentives. Competition is in general extrinsic because it encourages the performer to win and beat others, not to enjoy the intrinsic rewards of the activity.

Social psychological research has indicated that extrinsic rewards can lead to over justification and a subsequent reduction in intrinsic motivation. In one study demonstrating this effect, children who expected to be (and were) rewarded with a ribbon and a gold star for drawing pictures spent less time playing with the drawing materials in subsequent observations than children who were assigned to an unexpected reward condition and to children who received no extrinsic reward

Self-control

Self-control of motivation is increasingly understood as a subset of emotional intelligence; a person may be highly intelligent according to a more conservative definition (as measured by many intelligence tests), yet unmotivated to dedicate this intelligence to certain tasks. Yale School of Management professor Victor Vroom's "expectancy theory" provides an account of when people will decide whether to exert self control to pursue a particular goal. Drives and desires can be described as *a deficiency or need that activates behaviour that is aimed at a goal or an incentive.* These are thought to originate within the individual and may not require external stimuli to encourage the behaviour. Basic drives could be sparked by deficiencies such as hunger, which motivates a person to seek food; whereas more subtle drives might be the desire for praise and approval, which motivates a person to behave in a manner pleasing to others. By contrast, the rcle of extrinsic rewards and stimuli can be seen in the example of training animals by giving them treats when they perform a trick correctly. The treat motivates the animals to perform the trick consistently, even later when the treat is removed from the process.

Achievement Motivation

Over the years behavioral scientists have observed that some people have an intense need to achieve; others, perhaps the majority, do not seem to be as concerned about achievement. This phenomenon has fascinated David C. McClelland. For over twenty years he and his associates at Harvard University studied this urge to achieve. McClelland's research led him to believe that the need for achievement is a distinct human motive that can be distinguished from other needs. More important, the achievement motive can be isolated and assessed in any group.

Characteristics of People with a High Need for Achievement

McClelland illustrates some of these characteristics in describing a laboratory experiment. Participants were asked to throw rings over a peg from any distance they chose. Most people tended to throw at random-now close, now far away; but individuals with a high need for achievement seemed carefully to measure where they were most likely to get a sense of mastery—not too close to make the task ridiculously easy or too far away to make it impossible. They set moderately difficult but potentially achievable goals. In biology, this is known as the overload principle.

In weight lifting, for example, strength cannot be in creased by tasks that can be performed easily or that cannot be performed without injury to the organism. Strength can be increased by lifting weights that are difficult but realistic enough to stretch the muscles.

Do People with a High Need for Achievement Behave Like this all the Time?

Achievement-motivated people are not gamblers. They prefer to work on a problem rather than leave the outcome to chance. With managers, setting moderately difficult but potentially achievable goals may be translated into an attitude toward risks. Many people tend to be extreme in their attitude toward risks, either favoring wild speculative gambling or minimizing their exposure to losses.

- Gamblers seem to choose the big risk because the outcome is beyond their power and, therefore, they can easily rationalize away their personal responsibility if they lose.

- The conservative individual chooses tiny risks where the gain is small but secure, perhaps because there is little danger of anything going wrong for which that person might be blamed.
- Achievement-motivated people take the middle ground, preferring a moderate degree of risk because they feel their efforts and abilities will probably influence the outcome. In business, this aggressive realism is the mark of the successful entrepreneur.

Rewards and Achievement-motivated People

Another characteristic of achievement-motivated people is that they seem to be more concerned with personal achievement than with the rewards of success. They do not reject rewards, but the rewards are not as essential as the accomplishment itself. They get a bigger "kick" out of winning or solving a difficult problem than they get from any money or praise they receive.

Money, to achievement-motivated people, is valuable primarily as a measurement of their performance. It provides them with a means of assessing their progress and comparing their achievements with those of other people. They normally do not seek money for status or economic security.

Feedback

A desire by people with a high need for achievement to seek situations in which they get concrete feedback on how well they are doing is closely related to this concern for personal accomplishment. Consequently, achievement-motivated people are often found in sales jobs or as owners and managers of their own businesses. In addition to concrete feedback, the nature of the feedback is important to achievement-motivated people. They respond favorably to information about their work. They are not interested in comments about their personal characteristics, such as how cooperative or helpful they are.

- Affiliation-motivated people might want social or attitudinal feedback.
- Achievement-motivated people might want job-relevant feedback. They want to know the score.

Why do Achievement-motivated People Behave as they do?

McClelland claims it is because they habitually spend time thinking about doing things better. In fact, he has found that wherever people start to think in achievement terms, things start to happen.

Examples

College students with a high need for achievement will generally get better grades than equally bright students with weaker achievement needs.

- Achievement-motivated people tend to get more raises and are promoted faster because they are constantly trying to think of better ways of doing things.
- Companies with many such people grow faster and are more profitable.

McClelland has even extended his analysis to countries where he related the presence of a large percentage of achievement-motivated individuals to the national economic growth.

Stress

Stress is the individuals' perception of unpleasant or uncomfortable state.

TYPES OF STRESS

Frustration: Traffic jams, Examination, Language learning, Reaching goal

Conflict: High levels of anxiety, Depression, Physical symptoms

Change: Life, Behaviour, Negative changes

Pressure: It involves expectation or demands.

SOURCES OF STRESS

Personal

Short, Short hair, Colour, Irregular teeth , Excessively slim, Tall, Not good looking, Baldness, Voice (physical) Language Learning, Less Intelligence, Less Talents, Concentration , Attractive To The Opposite Sex, Lack Of Confident, Inferiority (Psychological)

Home Stress

Financial Problems, Children Not Studying Well, Conflict With Mother-In-Law or Daughter-In-Law And Neighbourhood, Others Are Not Sharing Work, Chronic Illness of Family Members, Not An Understanding Partner, Cooperation With Family Members.

Occupational Stress

More Work, Less Recognition and No Reward for More Work, Trouble Some Students or Colleagues, Less Time For Preparing Examination, Mark Scoring.

Society Stress

Corruption, Dowry System, Political Interference, Child Marriage, Caste, Religion, Conflict with Friend or Others.

Natural Stress

Earthquake, Floods, Droughts, Cyclone.

Identify the Sources of Stress in your Life

Stress management starts with identifying the sources of stress in your life. This isn't as easy as it sounds. Your true sources of stress aren't always obvious, and it's all too easy to overlook your own stress-inducing thoughts, feelings, and behaviors. Sure, you may know that you're constantly worried about work deadlines. But maybe it's your procrastination, rather than the actual job demands, that leads to deadline stress.

To identify your true sources of stress, look closely at your habits, attitude, and excuses:

- Do you explain away stress as temporary ("I just have a million things going on right now") even though you can't remember the last time you took a breather?
- Do you define stress as an integral part of your work or home life ("Things are always crazy around here") or as a part of your personality ("I have a lot of nervous energy, that's all").
- Do you blame your stress on other people or outside events, or view it as entirely normal and unexceptional?

Until you accept responsibility for the role you play in creating or maintaining it, your stress level will remain outside your control.

Start a Stress Journal

A stress journal can help you identify the regular stressors in your life and the way you deal with them. Each time you feel stressed; keep track of it in your journal. As you keep a daily log, you will begin to see patterns and common themes. Write down:

- What caused your stress (make a guess if you're unsure).
- How you felt, both physically and emotionally.
- How you acted in response.
- What you did to make yourself feel better.

Look at How you Currently Cope with Stress

Think about the ways you currently manage and cope with stress in your life. Your stress journal can help you identify them. Are your coping strategies healthy or unhealthy, helpful or unproductive? Unfortunately, many people cope with stress in ways that compound the problem.

These coping strategies may temporarily reduce stress, but they cause more damage in the long run:

- Smoking
- Drinking too much
- Overeating or undereating
- Zoning out for hours in front of the TV or computer
- Withdrawing from friends, family, and activities
- Using pills or drugs to relax
- Sleeping too much
- Procrastinating
- Filling up every minute of the day to avoid facing problems
- Taking out your stress on others (lashing out, angry outbursts, physical violence)

Learning Healthier Ways to Manage Stress

If your methods of coping with stress aren't contributing to your greater emotional and physical health, it's time to find healthier ones. There are many healthy ways to manage and cope with stress, but they all require change. You can either change the situation or change your reaction. When deciding which option to choose, it's helpful to think of the four as: avoid, alter, adapt, or accept.

Since everyone has a unique response to stress, there is no "one size fits all" solution to managing it. No single method works for everyone or in every situation, so experiment with different techniques and strategies. Focus on what makes you feel calm and in control.

Dealing with Stressful Situations: The Four A's

Change the situation:	Change your reaction:
• Avoid the stressor.	• Adapt to the stressor.
• Alter the stressor.	• Accept the stressor.

Stress Management Strategy 1: Avoid Unnecessary Stress

Not all stress can be avoided, and it's not healthy to avoid a situation that needs to be addressed. You may be surprised, however, by the number of stressors in your life that you can eliminate.

- *Learn how to say "no":* Know your limits and stick to them. Whether in your personal or professional life, refuse to accept added responsibilities when you're close to reaching them. Taking on more than you can handle is a surefire recipe for stress.
- *Avoid people who stress you out:* If someone consistently causes stress in your life and you can't turn the relationship around, limit the amount of time you spend with that person or end the relationship entirely.
- *Take control of your environment:* If the evening news makes you anxious, turn the TV off. If traffic's got you tense, take a longer but less-traveled route. If going to the market is an unpleasant chore, do your grocery shopping online.
- *Avoid hot-button topics:* If you get upset over religion or politics, cross them off your conversation list. If you repeatedly argue about the same subject with the same people, stop bringing it up or excuse yourself when it's the topic of discussion.
- *Pare down your to-do list:* Analyze your schedule, responsibilities, and daily tasks. If you've got too much on your plate, distinguish between the

"should" and the "musts." Drop tasks that aren't truly necessary to the bottom of the list or eliminate them entirely.

Stress Management Strategy 2: Alter the Situation

If you can't avoid a stressful situation, try to alter it. Figure out what you can do to change things so the problem doesn't present itself in the future. Often, this involves changing the way you communicate and operate in your daily life.

- ***Express your feelings instead of bottling them up:*** If something or someone is bothering you, communicate your concerns in an open and respectful way. If you don't voice your feelings, resentment will build and the situation will likely remain the same.
- ***Be willing to compromise:*** When you ask someone to change their behavior, be willing to do the same. If you both are willing to bend at least a little, you'll have a good chance of finding a happy middle ground.
- ***Be more assertive:*** Don't take a backseat in your own life. Deal with problems head on, doing your best to anticipate and prevent them. If you've got an exam to study for and your chatty roommate just got home, say up front that you only have five minutes to talk.
- ***Manage your time better:*** Poor time management can cause a lot of stress. When you're stretched too thin and running behind, it's hard to stay calm and focused. But if you plan ahead and make sure you don't overextend yourself, you can alter the amount of stress you're under.

Stress Management Strategy 3: Adapt to the Stressor

If you can't change the stressor, change yourself. You can adapt to stressful situations and regain your sense of control by changing your expectations and attitude.

- ***Reframe problems:*** Try to view stressful situations from a more positive perspective. Rather than fuming about a traffic jam, look at it as an opportunity to pause and regroup, listen to your favorite radio station, or enjoy some alone time.
- ***Look at the big picture:*** Take perspective of the stressful situation. Ask yourself how important it will be in the long run. Will it matter in a month? A year? Is it really worth getting upset over? If the answer is no, focus your time and energy elsewhere.
- ***Adjust your standards:*** Perfectionism is a major source of avoidable stress. Stop setting yourself up for failure by demanding perfection. Set reasonable standards for yourself and others, and learn to be okay with "good enough."
- ***Focus on the positive:*** When stress is getting you down, take a moment to reflect on all the things you appreciate in your life, including your own positive qualities and gifts. This simple strategy can help you keep things in perspective.

Adjusting Your Attitude

How you think can have a profound affect on your emotional and physical well-being. Each time you think a negative thought about yourself, your body reacts as if it were in the throes of a tension-filled situation. If you see good things about yourself, you are more likely to feel good; the reverse is also true. Eliminate words such as "always," "never," "should," and "must." These are telltale marks of self-defeating thoughts.

Stress Management Strategy 4: Accept the things you can't Change

Some sources of stress are unavoidable. You can't prevent or change stressors such as the death of a loved one, a serious illness, or a national recession. In such cases, the best way to cope with stress is to accept things as they are. Acceptance may be difficult, but in the long run, it's easier than railing against a situation you can't change.

- ***Don't try to control the uncontrollable:*** Many things in life are beyond our control—particularly the behavior of other people. Rather than stressing out over them, focus on the things you can control such as the way you choose to react to problems.
- ***Look for the upside:*** As the saying goes, "What doesn't kill us makes us stronger." When facing major challenges, try to look at them as opportunities for personal growth. If your own poor choices contributed to a stressful situation, reflect on them and learn from your mistakes.
- ***Share your feelings:*** Talk to a trusted friend or make an appointment with a therapist. Expressing what you're going through can be very cathartic, even if there's nothing you can do to alter the stressful situation.
- ***Learn to forgive:*** Accept the fact that we live in an imperfect world and that people make mistakes. Let go of anger and resentments. Free yourself from negative energy by forgiving and moving on.

Stress Management Strategy 5 : Make Time for Fun and Relaxation

Beyond a take-charge approach and a positive attitude, you can reduce stress in your life by nurturing yourself. If you regularly make time for fun and relaxation, you'll be in a better place to handle life's stressors when they inevitably come.

Healthy Ways to Relax and Recharge

- Go for a walk.
- Spend time in nature.

- Call a good friend.
- Sweat out tension with a good workout.
- Write in your journal.
- Take a long bath.
- Light scented candles.
- Savor a warm cup of coffee or tea.
- Play with a pet.
- Work in your garden.
- Get a massage.
- Curl up with a good book.
- Listen to music.
- Watch a comedy.

Don't get so caught up in the hustle and bustle of life that you forget to take care of your own needs. Nurturing yourself is a necessity, not a luxury.

- **Set aside relaxation time.** Include rest and relaxation in your daily schedule. Don't allow other obligations to encroach. This is your time to take a break from all responsibilities and recharge your batteries.
- **Connect with others.** Spend time with positive people who enhance your life. A strong support system will buffer you from the negative effects of stress.
- **Do something you enjoy every day.** Make time for leisure activities that bring you joy, whether it be stargazing, playing the piano, or working on your bike.
- **Keep your sense of humor.** This includes the ability to laugh at you. The act of laughing helps your body fight stress in a number of ways.

Learn the Relaxation Response

You can control your stress levels with relaxation techniques that evoke the body's relaxation response, a state of restfulness that is the opposite of the stress response. Regularly practicing these techniques will build your physical and emotional resilience, heal your body, and boost your overall feelings of joy and equanimity.

Stress Management Strategy: Adopt a Healthy Lifestyle

You can increase your resistance to stress by strengthening your physical health.

- *Exercise regularly:* Physical activity plays a key role in reducing and preventing the effects of stress. Make time for at least 30 minutes of exercise, three times per week. Nothing beats aerobic exercise for releasing pent-up stress and tension.
- *Eat a healthy diet:* Well-nourished bodies are better prepared to cope with stress, so be mindful of what you eat. Start your day right with breakfast, and keep your energy up and your mind clear with balanced, nutritious meals throughout the day.
- *Reduce caffeine and sugar:* The temporary "highs" caffeine and sugar provide often end in with a crash in mood and energy. By reducing the amount of coffee, soft drinks, chocolate, and sugar snacks in your diet, you'll feel more relaxed and you'll sleep better.
- *Avoid alcohol, cigarettes, and drugs:* Self-medicating with alcohol or drugs may provide an easy escape from stress, but the relief is only temporary. Don't avoid or mask the issue at hand; deal with problems head on and with a clear mind.
- *Get enough sleep:* Adequate sleep fuels your mind, as well as your body. Feeling tired will increase your stress because it may cause you to think irrationally.

CHAPTER

4

The Human Concept of Cognitive

The self is a key construct in several schools of psychology, broadly referring to the cognitive and affective representation of one's identity. The earliest formulation of the self in modern psychology from the distinction between the self as *I*, the subjective knower, and the self as *me*, the object that is known. Current views of the self in psychology diverge greatly from this early conception, positioning the self as playing an integral part in human motivation, cognition, affect, and social identity. Self following from John Locke has been seen as a product of episodic memory but research upon those with amnesia find they have a coherent sense of self based upon preserved conceptual autobiographical knowledge. It may be the case that we can now usefully attempt to ground experience of self in a neural process with cognitive consequences, which will give us insight into the elements of which the complex multiply situated selves of modern identity are composed.

The Cognitive and Immunological Self

The biological phenomenon that most resembles the human concept of selfhood, is perhaps, immunological response. © Nualláin analyses the subject-object distinction in quantum mechanics, consciousness studies, and philosophy before concluding that the immunological metaphor is informative. He adduces simulated and experimental data suggesting that our construction of self arises from ego-alien material arising in samples taken at intervals in the range of a tenth of a second from the much faster processes occurring continually in the brain. In related work, he argues that the meditative process arrests this sampling process and, if intermittently, allows identification with the process of pure observation, subjectivity itself. In his cognitive science textbook "The Search for Mind" this argument is presented is a genetic epistemology context; the Biosemiotics journal, Vol. 3 (2010) features a paper making explicit the dialogue with spiritual and philosophical traditions hinted at in © Nualláin(2006). Briefly, this work combines the classical notion of the "interpreter", the left hemisphere process that continues to narrate on our experience in a way that predicates agency and consistency of ourselves, with the immunological idea.

Kohut's Formulation

Heinz Kohut initially proposed a bipolar self compromising two systems of narcissistic perfection: *(1) a system of ambitions and, (2) a system of ideals.* Kohut called the pole of ambitions the *narcissistic self* (later, the *grandiose self*), while the pole of ideals was designated the *idealized parental imago*. According to Kohut, these poles of the self represented natural progressions in the psychic life of infants and toddlers.

Kohut argued that when the child's ambitions and exhibitionistic strivings were chronically frustrated, arrests in the grandiose self led to the preservation of a false, expansive sense of self that could manifest outwardly in the visible grandiosity of the frank narcissist, or remain hidden from view, unless discovered in a narcissistic therapeutic transference (or *self object transference*) that would expose these primitive grandiose fantasies and strivings. Kohut termed this form of transference mirror *transference*. In this transference, the strivings of the grandiose self are mobilized and the patient attempts to use the therapist to gratify these strivings. Kohut proposed that arrests in the pole of ideals occurred when the child suffered chronic and excessive disappointment over the failings of early idealized figures. Deficits in the pole of ideals were associated with the development of an idealizing transference to the therapist who becomes associated with the patient's primitive fantasies of omnipotent parental perfection.

Kohut believed that narcissistic injuries were inevitable and, in any case, necessary to temper ambitions and ideals with realism through the experience of more manageable frustrations and disappointments. It was the chronicity and lack of recovery from these injuries (arising from a number of possible causes) that he regarded as central to the preservation of primitive self systems untempered by realism. By 1984, Kohut's observation of patients led him to propose two additional forms of transference associated with self deficits: *(1) the twin ship and, (2) the merger transference.* In his later years, Kohut believed that self object needs were both present and quite varied in normal individuals, as well as in narcissistic individuals. To be clear, self objects are not external persons. Kohut and Wolf, 1978 explain:

> *"Self objects are objects which we experience as part of our self; the expected control over them is, therefore, closer to the concept of control which a grownup expects to have over his own body and mind than to the concept of control which he expects to have over others. (p. 413)"*

Kohut's notion of the self can be difficult to grasp because it is experience-distant, although it is posited based upon experience-near observation of the therapeutic transference. Kohut relied heavily on empathy as a method of observation. Specifically, the clinician's observations of his or her own feelings in the transference help the clinician see things from the subjective view of the patient—to experience the world in ways that are closer to the way the patient experiences it.

(Note: Kohut did not regard empathy as curative. Empathy is a method of observation).

Self (philosophy)

Self is broadly defined as the essential qualities that make a person distinct from all others. The task in philosophy is defining what these qualities are, and there have been a number of different approaches. The "self" is the idea of a unified being which is the source of consciousness. Moreover, this self is the agent responsible for the thoughts and actions of an individual to which they are ascribed. It is a substance, which therefore endures through time; thus, the thoughts and actions at different moments of time may pertain to the same self. As the notion of subject, the "self" has been harshly criticized by Nietzsche at the end of the 19th century, on behalf of what Gilles Deleuze would call a "becoming-other".

Philosophical Definition

Most philosophical definitions of self are expressed in the first person, as with Descartes, Locke, Hume, and William James. A third person definition does not refer to specific mental qualia but instead strives for objectivity and operationally. To another person, the self of one individual is exhibited in the conduct and discourse of that individual. Therefore, the intentions of another individual can only be inferred indirectly from something emanating from that individual. The particular characteristics of the self determine its identity.

Concepts of Self, Self as an Illusion

In spirituality, and especially nondual, mystical and eastern meditative traditions, the human being is often conceived as being in the illusion of individual existence, and separateness from other aspects of creation. This "sense of doership" or sense of individual existence is that part which believes it is the human being, and believes it must fight for itself in the world, is ultimately unaware and unconscious of its own true nature. The ego is often associated with mind and the sense of time, which compulsively thinks in order to be assured of its future existence, rather than simply knowing its own self and the present. The spiritual goal of many traditions involves the dissolving of the ego, allowing self-knowledge of one's own true nature to become experienced and enacted in the world. This is variously known as enlightenment, nirvana, presence, and the "here and now".

Self-knowledge

Lao Tzu, in his *Tao Te Ching*, says "Knowing others is wisdom. Knowing the self is enlightenment. Mastering others requires force. Mastering the self requires strength." Adi Shankaracharya, in his commentary on Bhagavad Gita says "Self-knowledge alone eradicates misery". "Self-knowledge alone is the means to the highest bliss."."Absolute perfection is the consummation of Self-knowledge."

Self as an Activity

Aristotle, following Plato, defined the soul as the core essence of a being, but argued against its having a separate existence. For instance, if a knife had a soul, the act of cutting would be that soul, because 'cutting' is the essence of what it is to be a knife. Unlike Plato and the religious traditions, Aristotle did not consider the soul as some kind of separate, ghostly occupant of the body (just as we cannot separate the activity of cutting from the knife). As the soul, in Aristotle's view, is an activity of the body, it cannot be immortal (when a knife is destroyed, the cutting stops). More precisely, the soul is the "first activity" of a living body. This is a state, or a potential for actual, or 'second', activity. "The axe has an edge for cutting" was, for Aristotle, analogous to "humans have bodies for rational activity," and the potential for rational activity thus constituted the essence of a human soul. Aristotle used his concept of the soul in many of his works; the *De Anima*

(On the Soul) provides a good place to start to gain more understanding of his views. Aristotle also believed that there were four sections of the soul. The four sections are calculative part, the scientific part on the rational side used for making decisions and the desiderative part and the vegetative part on the irrational side responsible for identifying our needs.

Self Independent of the Senses

While he was imprisoned in a castle, Avicenna wrote his famous "Floating Man" thought experiment to demonstrate human self-awareness and the substantiality of the soul. His "Floating Man" thought experiment tells its readers to imagine themselves suspended in the air, isolated from all sensations, which includes no sensory contact with even their own bodies. He argues that, in this scenario, one would still have self-consciousness. He thus concludes that the idea of the self is not logically dependent on any physical thing, and that the soul should not be seen in relative terms, but as a primary given, a substance. This argument was later refined and simplified by René Descartes in epistemic terms when he stated: "I can abstract from the supposition of all external things, but not from the supposition of my own consciousness."

Bundle Theory of Self

David Hume pointed out that we tend to think that we are the same person we were five years ago. Though we have changed in many respects, the same person appears present as was present then. We might start thinking about which features can be changed without changing the underlying self. Hume, however, denies that there is a distinction between the various features of a person and the mysterious self that supposedly bears those features. When we start introspecting, "we are never intimately conscious of anything but a particular perception; man is a bundle or collection of different perceptions which succeed one another with an inconceivable rapidity and are in perpetual flux and movement".

It is plain, that in the course of our thinking, and in the constant revolution of our ideas, our imagination runs easily from one idea to any other that resembles it, and that this quality alone is to the fancy a sufficient bond and association. It is likewise evident that as the senses, in changing their objects, are necessitated to change them regularly, and take them as they lie contiguous to each other, the imagination must by long custom acquire the same method of thinking, and run along the parts of space and time in conceiving its objects."

On Hume's view, these perceptions do not belong to anything. Rather, Hume compares the soul to a commonwealth, which retains its identity not by virtue of some enduring core substance, but by being composed of many different, related, and yet constantly changing elements. The question of personal identity then becomes a matter of characterizing the loose cohesion of one's personal experience. (Note that in the Appendix to the *Treatise*, Hume said mysteriously that he was dissatisfied with his account of the self, yet he never returned to the issue.) This view is very similar to that in Buddhism.

Self-enquiry and Self-surrender

Ramana Maharshi's primary teachings documented in the book *Nan Yar* (*Who am I*) state:

- Enquire into the source of the "I" Consciousness by asking "Who am I". The source or seat of "I" consciousness is the true self.
- Self itself is the world; Self itself is 'I'; Self itself is God; all is the Supreme Self (*siva swarupam*)

Although his primary teaching was self-enquiry, he was also known to have advised the use of self-surrender (to one's Deity or Guru) as an alternative means, which would ultimately converge in to the path of Self-Enquiry.

Self as a Narrative Center of Gravity

Daniel Dennett has a deflationary theory of the self. Selves are not physically detectable. Instead, they are a kind of convenient fiction, like a center of gravity, which are convenient as a way of solving physics problems, although they need not correspond to anything tangible—the center of gravity of a hoop is a point in thin air. People constantly tell themselves stories to make sense of their world, and they feature in the stories as a character, and that convenient but fictional character is the self.

The Buddha

The Buddha in particular attacked all attempts to conceive of a fixed self, while stating that holding the view "I have no self" is also mistaken. This is an example of the middle way charted by the Buddh

Johari Window

An empty Johari window, with the "Rooms" arranged clockwise, starting with Room 1 at the top left.

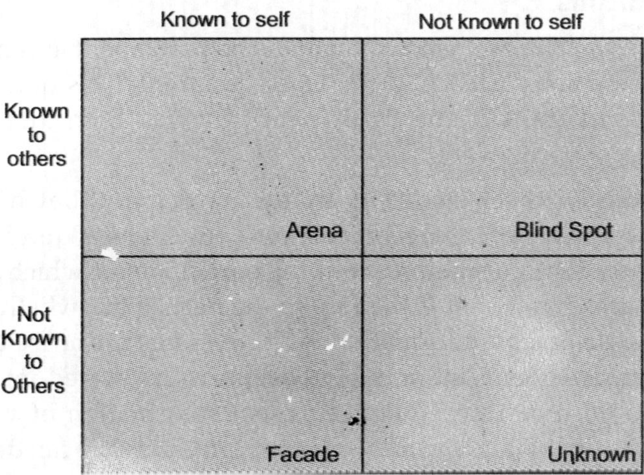

A *Johari window* is a cognitive psychological tool created by Joseph Luft and Harry Ingham in 1955 in the United States, used to help people better understand their interpersonal communication and relationships. It is used primarily in self-help groups and corporate settings as a heuristic exercise. When performing the exercise, the subject is given a list of 55 adjectives and picks five or six that they feel describe their own personality. Peers of the subject are then given the same list, and each pick five or six adjectives that describe the subject. These adjectives are then mapped onto a grid.

Charles Handy calls this concept the Johari House with four rooms. Room 1 is the part of ourselves that we see and others see. Room 2 is the aspect that others see but we are not aware of. Room 3 is the most mysterious room in that the unconscious or subconscious bit of us is seen by neither ourselves nor others. Room 4 is our private space, which we know but keep from others. The concept is clearly related to the ideas propounded in the Myers-Briggs Type Indicator programme, which in turn derive from theories about the personality first explored by the pioneering psychologist Carl Jung.

Quadrants

Adjectives that are selected by both the participant and his or her peers are placed into the *Open* quadrant. This quadrant represents traits of the participant of which both they and their peers are aware.

Adjectives selected only by the participant, but not by any of their peers, are placed into the *Hidden* quadrant, representing information about the participant of which their peers are unaware. It is then up to the participant whether or not to disclose this information. Adjectives that are not selected by the participant but only by their peers are placed into the *Blind Spot* quadrant. These represent information of which the participant is not aware, but others are, and they can decide whether and how to inform the individual about these *"blind spots"*.

Adjectives which were not selected by either the participant or their peers remain in the *Unknown* quadrant, representing the participant's behaviors or motives which were not recognized by anyone participating. This may be because they do not apply, or because there is collective ignorance of the existence of said trait.

Building Positive Attitude

Definition: A positive mental attitude is believing, accepting, hoping and working toward a good result in every situation. A positive mental attitude is constructive, while a negative mental attitude is destructive. It means spending creative energies on finding ways that things can be done rather than exhausting emotional and mental powers dwelling on the ways things cannot be done. It means turning a problem into a solution. It means developing what I call THOUGHT *Displacement*.

Let me explain... When you have a negative thought in your mind and it is nagging and pulling you down. What is really happening is that you are focusing on the thing you do not want to happen and in doing so you are, you are in fact focusing on the catastrophe and not the solution! Thought displacement changes all of that; but it requires discipline and imagination. So, let me share with you 5 steps to developing a positive mental attitude:

1. Imagine, visualize and keep thinking of things that you would like or prefer to happen for your problem: Imagine your problem is SOLVED. Use your imagination... you can do it. For example... if you are fearful that your project or presentation will fail, just remove those thoughts. Imagine and visualize your million dollar marketing presentation went excellently... and you CLOSED that deal!! Imagine earning $500 per day online... and your mind will think only of solutions to difficult problems. When the negative thought returns, challenge it and replace it with a solution.

2. Pursue wisdom. Have a habit of always learning: Seek wisdom... pursue it. If it means reaching out for help from a wiser person or friend, just ASK for help. Read to find if others have also faced similar problems. We can learn from others. Read life stories of people who have overcome incredible difficulties. When a negative mental attitude dwells in your mind, go read a book about real life stories of people overcome. In so doing, you relate positively that they not only survived but they went on to WIN!

3. Affirm out loud daily with a positive attitude: Say aloud to yourself "I will solve my problem today" or "I will earn $500/day in my online business". You could write down your affirmations in a notebook which tells you clearly what you are going to do. If you are facing a "low self-esteem" problem, affirm who you are and what relationships, responsibilities you have for my life goals. With this daily check, you will keep being positive and highly motivated. Alternatively, record an audio recording of yourself, or find a recording that will help you to affirm your goals, responsibilities and self esteem daily.

4. Have a great attitude! Act and behave motivated even if you do not feel like it: Quite often we let our subconscious mind dictate our attitudes and take us off the right track. Have you heard that "Your *attitude* determines your *altitude* in life". Keep a right attitude. The key for high achievers and highly motivated individuals is their attitude. Although it may seems difficult, remember to keep a right attitude... doing what is right; acting and behaving motivated even in difficult situations. Eventually, our minds and spirits will respond positively.

5. Do something so that your mental or physical resources can be stretched: When you are dwelling on negative thoughts, does something so that you're mental or physical resources can be stretched? Go for a swim or jog. Learn to play a musical instrument, or cook up a storm in the kitchen preparing dinner for the whole family! Learn a new sport like golf or scuba diving, or riding a horse!! Learn to blog... if you do not have a blog... why not!! You will find your mind and body refreshed by the experiences.

Look for the positive in every situation. If you do, you will definitely see the light (the solution) and find opportunities for growth, learning and experience. Remember to use affirmations like:

- I can do it
- I will succeed
- It's an opportunity
- I will find out
- It will work
- It will help me grow

During childhood, we form attitudes that last a lifetime. Undoubtedly, it would be a lot easier and better to have acquired a positive attitude during our formative years. Does that mean if we acquire a negative attitude, whether by design or by default, we are stuck with it? of course not. Can we change? Yes. Is it easy? Absolutely not. How do you build and maintain a positive attitude?

¨ Become aware of the principles that build a positive attitude;

¨ Desire to be positive; and

¨ Cultivate the discipline and dedication to practice those principles as adults, regardless of our environment, education and experience, who is responsible for our attitude? We are. We have to accept responsibility some time in our lives. We blame everyone and everything but ourselves. It is up to us to choose our attitude every morning. As adults, we need to accept responsibility for our behavior and actions. People with negative attitudes will blame the whole world, their parents, teachers, spouse, the economy and the government for their failures. You have to get away from the past. Dust yourself off, get back into the mainstream. Put your dreams together and move forward. Thinking of the positive things that are true, honest and good, will put us in a positive state of mind. If we want to build and maintain a positive attitude, we need to consciously practice the following steps:

Step 1: Change Focus, Look for the Positive: We need to become good finders. We need to focus on the positive in life. Let's start looking for what is right in a person or situation instead of looking for what is wrong. Because of our conditioning, we are so attuned to finding fault and looking for what is wrong that we forget to see the positive picture. Even in paradise, fault finders will find faults. Most people find what they are looking for. If they are looking for friendship, happiness and the positive, that is what they get. If they are looking for fights or indifference, then that is what they get. Caution looking for the positive does not mean overlooking faults.

Step 2: Make a Habit of Doing It Now: We have all procrastinated at some time in our lives. I know I have, only to have regretted it later. Procrastination leads to a negative attitude. The habit of procrastination fatigues you more than the effort it takes to do it. A completed task is fulfilling and energizing; an incomplete task drains energy like a leak from a tank. If you want to build and maintain a positive attitude, get into the habit of living in the present and doing it now.

Step 3: Develop an Attitude of Gratitude: Count your blessings, not your troubles. Take time to smell the roses. It is not uncommon to hear that someone, because of an accident or illness, became blind or paralyzed but won a million dollars in settlement. How many of us would like to trade places with that person? Not many. We are so focused on complaining about things we don't have that we lose sight of the things we have. There is a lot to be thankful for. When I say count your blessings, not your troubles, the message is not to become complacent. If complacence was the message you got, then I would be guilty of faulty communication and you of selective listening.

Step 4: Get into a Continuous Education Program: Let's get some myths out of the way. It is a general belief that we get educated in schools and colleges. I run seminars in many different countries and ask my audiences all the time, "Do we really get educated in schools and colleges?" Generally, there is a consensus that some do but most don't. We receive a lot of information in schools and colleges. Don't get me wrong. We do need information to be educated. But we need to know the true meaning of education.

Intellectual education influences the head and values based education influences the heart. In fact, education that does not train the heart can be dangerous. If we want to build character in our offices, homes and society, we must achieve a minimum level of moral and ethical literacy. Education that builds fundamental traits of character—such as honesty, compassion, courage, persistence and responsibility—is absolutely essential. We don't need more academic education; we need more values education. I would stress that a person who is morally educated will be a lot better equipped to move up in life or succeed than a morally bankrupt person with excellent academic qualifications. Character building and teaching values and ethics come in the formative years because a child is not born with this knowledge.

Step 5: Build a Positive Self-Esteem: What is Self-Esteem? Self-esteem is the way we feel about ourselves. When we feel good within, our performance goes up, our relationships improve both at home and at work. The world looks nicer. What is the reason? There is a direct correlation between feeling and behavior. How Do We Build Positive Self-Esteem? If you want to build positive self-esteem quickly, one of the fastest ways is to do something for others who cannot repay you in cash or kind.

Step 6: Stay Away from Negative Influences: Today's teenagers learn from adult behavior and the media. They face peer pressure. Peer pressure is not just limited to teenagers; it is also prevalent in adults. It shows a lack of self-esteem when people do not have the courage to say "No, thank you," and stay away from negative influences; such as Negative people, Smoking, Drug Abuse, Drinking excessive Alcohol,Pornography,Negative Movies and Television Programs, Profanity, to mention just but few.

Step 7: Learn to Like the Things That Need to be done: Some things need to be done whether we like them or not; for example, mothers caring for their young. They may not be fun and games, and may even be painful. But if we learn to like the task, the impossible becomes possible.St. Francis of Assisi once said "Start by doing what is necessary, then what is possible, and suddenly you are doing the impossible."

Step 8: Start Your Day with a Positive: Read or listen to something positive first thing in the morning. After a good night's sleep we are relaxed and our subconscious is receptive. It sets the tone for the day, and puts us in the right frame of mind to make every day a positive day. In order to bring about change, we need to make a conscious effort Andre committed to make positive thoughts and behavior part of our lives. Practice having positive thoughts and behavior daily until they become a habit. William James of Harvard University said, "If you are going to change your life, you need to start immediately and do it flamboyantly."

Self-esteem

The term self-esteem comes from a Greek word meaning "reverence for self." The "self" part of self-esteem pertains to the values, beliefs and attitudes that we hold about ourselves. The "esteem" part of self-esteem describes the value and worth that one gives oneself. Simplistically self-esteem is the acceptance of us for whom and what we are at any given time in our lives.

Self-esteem is a term used in psychology to reflect a person's overall evaluation or appraisal of his or her own worth. Self-esteem encompasses beliefs (for example, "I am competent" or "I am incompetent") and emotions such as triumph, despair, pride and shame. A person's self-esteem may be reflected in their behaviour, such as in assertiveness, shyness, confidence or caution. Self-esteem can apply specifically to a particular dimension (for example, "I believe I am a good writer, and feel proud of that in particular") or have global extent (for example, "I believe I am a good person, and feel proud of myself in general"). Psychologists usually regard self-esteem as an enduring personality characteristic ("trait" self-esteem), though normal, short-term variations ("state" self-esteem) also exist.

Synonyms or near-synonyms of self-esteem include: self-worth, self-regard, self-respect, self-love (which can express overtones of self-promotion), and self-integrity. Self-esteem is distinct from self-confidence and self-efficacy, which involve beliefs about ability and future performance.

Definitions

Given its long and varied history, the term has had no less than three major types of definition, each of which has generated its own tradition of research, findings, and practical applications:

1. The original definition presents self-esteem as a ratio found by dividing one's successes in areas of life of importance to a given individual by the failures in them or one's "success/pretensions". Problems with this approach come from making self-esteem contingent upon success: this implies inherent instability because failure can occur at any moment.
2. In the mid 1960s Morris Rosenberg and social-learning theorists defined self-esteem in terms of a stable sense of personal worth or worthiness, (see Rosenberg self esteem scale). This became the most frequently used definition for research, but involves problems of boundary-definition, making self-esteem

indistinguishable from such things as narcissism or simple bragging.

3. Nathaniel Branden in 1969 briefly defined self-esteem as "...the experience of being competent to cope with the basic challenges of life and being worthy of happiness". This two-factor approach, as some have also called it, provides a balanced definition that seems to be capable of dealing with limits of defining self-esteem primarily in terms of competence or worth alone.

Branden's (1969) description of self-esteem includes the following primary properties:

1. self-esteem as a basic human need, *i.e.,* "...it makes an essential contribution to the life process", "...is indispensable to normal and healthy self-development, and has a value for survival."
2. self-esteem as an automatic and inevitable consequence of the sum of individuals' choices in using their consciousness
3. something experienced as a part of, or background to, all of the individuals thoughts, feelings and actions.

Self esteem is a concept of personality, for it to grow, we need to have self worth, and this self worth will be sought from embracing challenges that result in the showing of success.

Compare the usage of terms such as *self-love* or *self-confidence*

Implicit self-esteem refers to a person's disposition to evaluate themselves positively or negatively in a spontaneous, automatic, or unconscious manner. It contrasts with *explicit self-esteem,* which entails more conscious and reflective self-evaluation. Both explicit self-esteem and implicit self-esteem are subtypes of self-esteem proper.

Implicit self-esteem is assessed using indirect measures of cognitive processing. These include the Name Letter Task and the Implicit Association Test. Such indirect measures are designed to reduce awareness of, or control of, the process of assessment. When used to assess implicit self-esteem, they feature stimuli designed to represent the self, such as personal pronouns (*e.g.*, "I") or letters in one's name.

Measurement

For the purposes of empirical research, psychologists typically assess self-esteem by a self-report inventory yielding a quantitative result. They establish the validity and reliability of the questionnaire prior to its use. Researchers are becoming more interested in measures of implicit self-esteem. Whereas popular lore recognizes just "high" self-esteem and "low" self-esteem, the Rosenberg Self-Esteem Scale (1965) and the Coopersmith Self-Esteem Inventory (1967/1981) both quantify it in more detail, and feature among the most widely used systems for measuring self-esteem. The Rosenberg test usually uses a ten-question battery scored on a four-point response system that requires participants to indicate their level of agreement with a series of statements about themselves. The Coopersmith Inventory uses a 50-question battery over a variety of topics and asks subjects whether they rate someone as similar or dissimilar to themselves.

Theories

Many early theories suggested that self-esteem is a basic human need or motivation. American psychologist Abraham Maslow, for example, included self-esteem in his hierarchy of needs. He described two different forms of esteem: the need for respect from others and the need for self-respect, or inner self-esteem. Respect from others entails recognition, acceptance, status, and appreciation, and was believed to be more fragile and easily lost than inner self-esteem. According to Maslow, without the fulfillment of the self-esteem need, individuals will be driven to seek it and unable to grow and obtain self-actualization.

Modern theories of self-esteem explore the reasons why humans are motivated to maintain a high regard for themselves. Sociometer theory maintains that self-esteem evolved to check one's level of status and acceptance in ones' social group. According to terror management theory, self-esteem serves a protective function and reduces anxiety about life and death.

Quality and Level of Self-esteem

Level and quality of self-esteem, though correlated, remain distinct. Level-wise, one can exhibit high but fragile self-esteem (as in narcissism) or low but stable self-esteem (as in humility). However, investigators can indirectly assess the quality of self-esteem in several ways:

1. in terms of its constancy over time (stability)
2. in terms of its independence of meeting particular conditions (non-contingency)
3. in terms of its ingrained nature at a basic psychological level (implicitness or automatized).

Humans have portrayed the dangers of excessive self-esteem and the advantages of more humility since at least the development of Greek tragedy, which typically showed the results of hubris.

Self-esteem, Grades and Relationships

From the late 1970s to the early 1990s many Americans assumed as a matter of course that students' self-esteem acted as a critical factor in the grades that they earn in school, in their relationships with their peers, and in their later success in life. Given this assumption, some American groups created programs which aimed to increase the self-esteem of students. Until the 1990s little peer-reviewed and controlled research took place on this topic.

The concept of self-improvement has undergone dramatic change since 1911, when Ambrose Bierce mockingly defined self-esteem as "an erroneous appeasement." Good and bad character is now known as "personality differences". Rights have replaced responsibilities. The research on ego centrism and ethnocentrism that informed discussion of human growth and development in the mid-20th century is ignored; indeed, the terms themselves are considered politically incorrect. A revolution has taken place in the vocabulary of self. Words that imply responsibility or accountability-self-criticism, self-denial, self-discipline, self-control, self-effacement, self-mastery, self-reproach, and self-sacrifice-are no longer in fashion. The language most in favor is that which exalts the self - self-expression, self-assertion, self-indulgence, self-realization, self-approval, self-acceptance, self-love, and the ubiquitous self-esteem. Peer-reviewed research undertaken since then has not validated previous assumptions. Recent research indicates that inflating students' self-esteem in and of itself has no positive effect on grades. One study has shown that inflating self-esteem by itself can actually decrease grades.

High self-esteem correlates highly with self-reported happiness. However, it is not clear which, if either, necessarily leads to the other. Additionally, self-esteem has been found to be related to forgiveness in close relationships, in that people with high self-esteem will be more forgiving than people with low self-esteem. The relationship involving self-esteem and academic results does not signify that high self-esteem contributes to high academic results. It simply means that high self- esteem may be accomplished due to high academic performance.

THE POWER OF THE SUBCONSCIOUS MIND

Subconscious

The term *subconscious* is used in many different contexts and has no single or precise definition. This greatly limits its significance as a meaning-bearing concept, and in consequence the word tends to be avoided in academic and scientific settings.

In everyday speech and popular writing, however, the term is very commonly encountered. There it will be employed to refer to a supposed 'layer' or 'level' of mentation (or/and perception) located in some sense 'beneath' conscious awareness—though, again, the notion's dependence upon informal 'folk-psychological' models that remain vague means that the precise nature and properties of this 'underlying' layer are either never made explicit or possess an *ad hoc* quality. At different times, references to the 'subconscious' as an agency may credit it with various abilities and powers that exceed those possessed by consciousness: the 'subconscious' may apparently remember, perceive and determine things beyond the reach or control of the conscious mind. The idea of the 'subconscious' as a powerful or potent agency has allowed the term to become prominent in the New Age and self-help literatures, in which investigating or controlling its supposed knowledge or power is seen as advantageous. The 'subconscious' may also be supposed to contain (thanks to the influence of the psychoanalytic tradition) any number of primitive or otherwise disavowed instincts, urges, desires and thoughts.

The word 'subconscious' is an anglicised version of the French *subconscient* as coined by the psychologist Pierre Janet. Janet himself saw the *subconscient* as active in hypnotic suggestion and as an area of the psyche to which ideas would be consigned through a process that involved a 'splitting' of the mind and a restriction of the field of consciousness.

The 'Subconscious' and Psychoanalysis

Though lay persons commonly assume 'subconscious' to be a psychoanalytic term, this is not in fact the case. Sigmund Freud had explicitly condemned the word as long ago as 1915: "We shall also be right in rejecting the term 'sub consciousness' as incorrect and misleading". In later publications his objections were made clear: Thus, as Charles Rycroft has explained, 'subconscious' is a term "never used in psychoanalytic writings". And, in Peter Gay's words, use of 'subconscious' where 'unconscious' is meant is "a common and telling mistake" indeed, "when [the term] is employed to say something 'Freudian', it is proof that the writer has not read his Freud".

Freud's own terms for mentation taking place outside conscious awareness were *dash Unbewusste* (rendered by his translators as 'the Unconscious') and *dash Vorbewusste* ('the Preconscious'); informal use of the term 'subconscious' in this context thus creates confusion, as it fails to make clear which (if either!) is meant. The distinction is of significance because in Freud's formulation the Unconscious is 'dynamically' unconscious, the Preconscious merely 'descriptively' so: the contents of the Unconscious require special investigative techniques for their exploration, whereas something in the Preconscious is unrepressed and can be recalled to consciousness by the simple direction of attention. The erroneous, pseudo-Freudan use of 'subconscious' and 'sub consciousness' has its precise equivalent in German, where the words inappropriately employed are *Unterbewusst* and *Unterbewusstsein.*

Subconscious Mind: Mind Power Tips by Steve Goldberg

For years, I have been absolutely fascinated with the power of the subconscious mind. It's power have made the sick healthy, the poor wealthy, and the sad happy. Those who understand and apply the methods for using the subconscious mind find themselves bathed in more abundance and joy than they could have ever imagined. In this article, I will explain two of the most powerful tips for harnessing and applying your subconscious mind power, to help you achieve far greater success than you have ever dreamed. As you might already be aware of, the subconscious mind is the seat of all memory, fears, phobias, behavioral patterns, habits, beliefs, and expectations. An astonishingly true fact is that only 2-4% of our day is controlled by our conscious mind, and the other 96-98% is all done by the subconscious. 96% of all your decisions, actions, thoughts and feelings are all done automatically, unconsciously by your subconscious mind.

It is amazing to think how much our subconscious mind does for us. It beats our heart, digests our food, and breathes for us all without any conscious effort. With all of the amazing things it does, our subconscious doesn't always do everything we want it to. Many people have realized that they have several bad habits of doing and thinking, and understand that in order to grow and prosper, those habits must be changed. But herein lies the problem most people face. How do you change the subconscious to promote success in all areas of life?

The answer is simple. You must harness the power of your subconscious mind. The first technique in order to do that is called suggestion. A suggestion is a passive statement given to the subconscious to either accept or reject. Hypnotists use the power of suggestibility to promote changes in their subjects. When a person is in a deeply relaxed state, their conscious mind is out of the way, and the gateway to the powers of subconscious is open. This is where true changes happen. In order to suggest the subconscious to change, the body and mind must be completely relaxed. A person must first have a reason to change, and accept the new suggestion. Then the suggestion for change may be given with intense emotion and desire so that the suggestion is firmly accepted.

In quick summary: Enter a deeply relaxed state—Subconscious is open to suggestion—Give suggestion and firmly accepts with intense emotion. The next subconscious mind power tip is repetition. If you are suggesting your subconscious to accept the idea of wealth in your life, using repetition can help firmly implant that idea quicker and easier. Our reptilian brain is highly receptive to ritual and repetition.

Repetition of an affirmation, or suggestion, such as "I am wealthy and successful" helps firmly implant the idea deeply into the subconscious mind. Over long periods of repetition, the suggestion will reshape thinking patterns, habits, and deeply held beliefs. The entire neuronal structure of your brain will begin change in order to promote the new idea of wealth and success. And once the idea is finally accepted without doubt or question, new worlds of possibilities begin to arise.

In summary: Repetition is the tool of suggestion—Repeat an affirmation for change in a deeply relaxed state—Repeat on regular intervals to help the reptilian brain accept the suggestion (repeat affirmation with intense emotion every morning, deeply relaxed, for 10 minutes for a period of one month or more). These two subconscious mind power tips can help you clear mental and emotional blockages in your life that are withholding your from your full potential. The power of suggestion to the subconscious mind, combined with ritualistic repetition is the ultimate key to unlocking your mind, and achieving all that you desire.

Have you ever read something that could make your life better, and then never put it to use? Most of us have done this. We read a book on real estate investing or speed-reading, and then we never make an offer on a house or do the scanning-exercises. Or we start, but don't continue. The potential value is lost. How, then, do you really benefit from the new mind power techniques that you'll learn in this course? How do you make permanent and ongoing changes? There are four parts to the process we're going to use. We start by getting the power of the subconscious mind working for you.

1. You need to really believe and "feel" that you can accomplish your goal of greater mind power. The power of your subconscious mind will work *against* you until you really expect results. More on how to get it working for you in a moment.

2. You need to learn to motivate yourself and re-motivate yourself as necessary. Understanding why you want greater mind power and imagining the benefits is a start. In future lessons, you'll learn specific methods of self-motivation.
3. You need to give your mind the right tools. In this case, these are specific tricks and techniques for clearer thinking, problem-solving, memory enhancement, and learning skills. These also include foods, supplements and environmental conditions that are conducive to mind power.
4. You need to develop habits that sustain your progress. Good habits-of-mind mean your subconscious will continue your progress even when your motivation is low. Good habits are crucial. I'll cover dozens of ways to boost your brainpower, but it's your habits that will ultimately make you more powerful.

Interpersonal Relationship

An *interpersonal relationship* is an association between two or more people that may range from fleeting to enduring. This association may be based on limerence, love and liking, regular business interactions, or some other type of social commitment. Interpersonal relationships take place in a great variety of contexts, such as family, friends, marriage, associates, work, clubs, neighborhoods, and churches. They may be regulated by law, custom, or mutual agreement, and are the basis of social groups and society as a whole. Although humans are fundamentally social creatures, interpersonal relationships are not always healthy. Examples of unhealthy relationships include abusive relationships and codependence.

A relationship is normally viewed as a connection between two individuals, such as a romantic or intimate relationship, or a parent-child relationship. Individuals can also have relationships with groups of people, such as the relation between a pastor and his congregation, an uncle and a family, or a mayor and a town. Finally, groups or even nations may have relations with each other, though this is a much broader domain than that covered under the topic of interpersonal relationships. See such articles as international relations for more information on associations between groups. Most scholarly work on relationships focuses on romantic partners in pairs or dyads. These intimate relationships are, however, only a small subset of interpersonal relationships.

These relationships usually involve some level of interdependence. People in a relationship tend to influence each other, share their thoughts and feelings, and engage in activities together. Because of this interdependence, most things that change or impact one member of the relationship will have some level of impact on the other member. The study of interpersonal relationships involves several branches of the social sciences, including such disciplines as sociology, psychology, anthropology, and social work.

Types

Close relationships are important for emotional wellbeing throughout the lifespan. Interpersonal relationships include kinship and family relations in which people become associated by genetics or consanguinity. These include such roles as father, mother, son, or daughter. Relationships can also be established by marriage, such as husband, wife, father-in-law, mother-in-law, uncle by marriage, or aunt by marriage. They may be formal long-term relationships recognized by law and formalized through public ceremony, such as marriage or civil union. They may also be informal long-term relationships such as loving relationships or romantic relationships with or without living together. In these cases the "other person" is often called lover, boyfriend, or girlfriend, as distinct from just a male or female friend, or "significant other". If the partners live together, the relationship may resemble marriage, with the parties possibly even called husband and wife. Scottish common law can regard such couples as actual marriages after a period of time. Long-term relationships in other countries can become known as common-law marriages, although they may have no special status in law. The term *mistress* may refer in a somewhat old-fashioned way to a female lover of an already married or unmarried man. A mistress may have the status of an "official mistress" (in French *maîtresse en titre*); as exemplified by the career of Madame de Pompadour.

The status of a relationship goes along with the way we communicate with them. Interpersonal relationships and communication is a two-way street, which needs to be clear by both ends. The way we communicate with our significant other is not the same as we communicate of our bosses or little brother. The transmission model of communication has five main parts according to Karen Reynolds essay: Information Source—where the message is produced Transmitter-where the message is encoded Channel- where the signal is carried Receiver-where the message is decoded Destination—where the message ends up However, noise can interfere with the channel and change the original message. This can relate to interpersonal relationships because the sender and receiver of messages need to be on the same of page of the context of the message so the message will not be taken the wrong way according to the Karen Reynolds. If the message is taken the wrong way, it could be detrimental to the relationship. Communication is a very important component to a successful relationship. As time goes on people's attitudes change because they have become more comfortable with a person. This could hurt the way the sender may send the message or the receiver interprets the message. In Daniel Chandler's essay, he states that no allowance is made for unequal power relations. In other words, he is saying that individuals will not always feel that the other person's ideas are valuable or creditable. In an interpersonal relationship point of view, a man could never believe what the girlfriend is saying according to his own standards, which would cause havoc in their communication. The way to interpret a person who communicates is different depending on the person; therefore, the transmission model is a hard way to partake in an interpersonal relationship, because the interpretation of a message can change at any time.

Friendships consist of mutual liking, trust, respect, and often even love and unconditional acceptance. They usually imply the discovery or establishment of similarities or common ground between the individuals. Internet friendships and pen-pals may take place at a considerable physical distance. Brotherhood and sisterhood can refer to individuals united in a common cause or having a common interest, which may involve formal membership in a club, organization, association, society, lodge, fraternity, or sorority. This type of interpersonal relationship relates to the comradeship of fellow soldiers in peace or war. Partners or co-workers in a profession, business, or common workplace also have a long term interpersonal relationship.

Soul mates are individuals intimately drawn to one another through a favorable meeting of minds and who find mutual acceptance and understanding with one another. Soulmates may feel themselves bonded together for a lifetime and hence may become sexual partners, but not necessarily. Casual relationships are sexual relationships extending beyond one-night stands that exclusively consist of sexual behavior. One can label the participants as "friends with benefits" or as friends "hooking up" when limited to sexual intercourse, or regard them as sexual partners in a wider sense. Platonic love is an affectionate relationship into which the sexual element does not enter, especially in cases where one might easily assume otherwise.

Development

Interpersonal relationships are dynamic systems that change continuously during their existence. Like living organisms, relationships have a beginning, a lifespan, and an end. They tend to grow and improve gradually, as people get to know each other and become closer emotionally, or they gradually deteriorate as people drift apart and form new relationships with others. One of the most influential models of relationship development was proposed by psychologist George Levinger. This model was formulated to describe heterosexual, adult romantic relationships, but it has been applied to other kinds of interpersonal relations as well. According to the model, the natural development of a relationship follows five stages:

1. *Acquaintance:* Becoming acquainted depends on previous relationships, physical proximity, first impressions, and a variety of other factors. If two people begin to like each other, continued interactions may lead to the next stage, but acquaintance can continue indefinitely.
2. *Buildup:* During this stage, people begin to trust and care about each other. The need for compatibility and such filtering agents as common background and goals will influence whether or not interaction continues.
3. *Continuation:* This stage follows a mutual commitment to a long term friendship, romantic relationship, or marriage. It is generally a long, relative stable period. Nevertheless, continued growth and development will occur during this time. Mutual trust is important for sustaining the relationship.
4. *Deterioration:* Not all relationships deteriorate, but those that do, tend to show signs of trouble. Boredom, resentment, and dissatisfaction may occur, and individuals may communicate less and avoid self-disclosure. Loss of trust and betrayals may take place as the downward spiral continues.
5. *Termination:* The final stage marks the end of the relationship, either by death in the case of a healthy relationship, or by separation.

Friendships may involve some degree of transitivity. In other words, a person may become a friend of an existing friend's friend. However, if two people have a sexual relationship with the same person, they may become competitors rather than friends. Accordingly, sexual behavior with the sexual partner of a friend may damage the friendship (see love triangle). Sexual relations between two friends tend to alter that relationship, either by "taking it to the next level" or by severing it. Sexual partners may also be classified as friends and the sexual relationship may either enhance or depreciate the friendship.

Legal sanction reinforces and regularizes marriages and civil unions as perceived "respectable" building-blocks of society. In the United States of America, for example, the de-criminalization of homosexual sexual relations in the Supreme Court decision, Lawrence v. Texas (2003) facilitated the mainstreaming of gay long-term relationships, and broached the possibility of the legalization of same-sex marriages in that country.

Tips for Improving Your Interpersonal Relations Skills

1 Techniques you can use to improve your interpersonal relations. How would you like to influence other people to develop a more positive attitude toward you? In this article you will discover several techniques you can use to improve your interpersonal relations with friends, family, coworkers, and employees. In fact, you can use these techniques to influence others to have a positive attitude toward you in just about any type of relationship.

I can't claim these techniques as my own. I got them from Dale Carnegie's classic book, How to Win Friends & Influence People. This book was first written in 1936, but Carnegie's ideas still hold true today. What follows is a brief synopsis of the main techniques outlined in the book. I highly recommend picking up a copy for your own collection to use for regular reference.

1. Don't criticize, condemn, or complain about people: There's no faster way create resentment toward you than to criticize or complain about a person. Instead of telling people they're doing something wrong, consider asking them questions to try to find out why they do what they do. Offer them an alternative in a way that comes across as trying to help. Show them how doing things the way you would like them done can benefit them or lead to reward.

2. Appreciate people: If you're normal, you're probably very quick to notice things you don't like about people. Maybe you sometimes even let people know when you don't like something. I'll let you in on a secret that can vastly improve your interpersonal relations-quickly: whenever you see someone, imagine them wearing a flashing sign on their chest that says **APPRECIATE ME, PLEASE!** Then, give them what they want. If you start appreciating the good things others are doing, they are much more likely to give you more good things to appreciate. Just make sure your appreciation is genuine. People will pick up on it if you're just feeding them a line, in which case you're better off having said nothing at all. You might have heard this saying when you were growing up: "If you can't say something nice, don't saying anything at all." Wise advice!

3. Solve your own problems by solving other people's problems: This relates to number one. If you would like someone to do something or act in a certain way, try to figure out how what you want might benefit him or her. This works especially well for people who work in sales. Instead of telling your potential clients how great your product is, ask them questions to find out what problems they might have. Once you know those issues, you can then work with your clients to help solve them. If they don't have a problem your product or service solves, then you know that you're not a good match. It saves a lot of time on chasing clients that were never really potential sales anyway.

As a side note, I've worked in sales and found this approach amazing. It really takes the pressure off both you and the client and it helps foster interpersonal relations built on trust. If you work in sales or deal with customers in any way, you might really enjoy this honest and open approach to selling. You can get more info here. I've worked through the material myself and it really made the whole sales process feel much more enjoyable and effective for both my clients and me.

4. Be genuinely interested in others: You'll make more friends by being interested in others than you ever will by trying to get people to be interested in you. This was touched on earlier, but it's worth repeating here. Not everyone will admit it, but the truth is, most people's favorite subject is themselves. Use this to your advantage. Become genuinely interested in other people. Ask them questions. Talk to them about things they're interested in. Put the focus on them. You'll quickly gain their friendship.

5. Smile: Smiles are infectious. They make others feel warm inside and warmer toward you. Force yourself to do it if you have to because it will ultimately make you feel better too. Try it right now: just smile!

6. Be a good listener: This goes back to the principle of focusing on the other person. Listen more than you speak and encourage others to talk about them and you'll quickly develop good interpersonal relations with them.

7. Make others feel important: If someone is important to you in any way, tell them so! This goes for any type of interpersonal relationship including your spouse, kids, employees, coworkers, your friends, family-anyone! People like to feel important. Give them what they want and they will love you for it. Again, it's important that you do this with sincerity. People can easily tell when you're just dishing something out for personal gain. Mean it when you say it.

8. Avoid arguing, and understand that you really aren't always right: When two people argue, neither one is really listening to the other. You'll be better off to try and remain calm and listen to the other person's thoughts. Then take some time to consider them. Maybe you're not right! And if you are right, telling someone else will only make them resentful. Be tactful in your approach and consider the other person's feelings. Try asking yourself how you would feel in their situation.

9. If you're wrong, admit it: You can really harm your interpersonal relations if you refuse to admit when you're wrong. It's frustrating for others and it damages their trust in you. If you're wrong, or you made a mistake, admit it. This will quickly clear the air and allow everyone to move on.

10. Save your anger: If you approach someone in anger, their defenses immediately go up and your discussion will go nowhere. If you have a problem with someone that needs to be sorted out, approach that person calmly. Ask them if you can sit down with them to work on an amicable solution for both of you. Everyone thinks more clearly when they're calm.

11. Suggest, don't tell: Interpersonal relations are strained when you tell someone how to do something or how to think. People like to come up with their own beliefs or opinions of how to do things. Instead, try offering suggestions. Suggestions leave people more open to considering your idea rather than stubbornly defending their position.

There are more areas covered in How to Win Friends & Influence People. But these main points should be enough to get you a long way in your own interpersonal relations. In general, people will have a more positive attitude toward you in record time. Try using one new technique each week and see how differently people start responding to you.

Building Positive Personality

Elbert Hubbard once said; "Responsibilities gravitate to the person who can shoulder them." This article will highlight the steps to building a positive personality, the steps are:

Step 1: Accept Responsibility: When people accept additional responsibility they are actually giving themselves a promotion. Responsible behavior is to accept accountability and that represents maturity. Acceptance of responsibility is a reflection of our attitude and the environment we operate in. Most people are quick to take credit for what goes right but very few would accept responsibility when things go wrong. A person who does not accept responsibility is not absolved from being responsible. Our objective is to cultivate responsible behavior. Responsible behavior should be inculcated right from childhood. It cannot be taught without a certain degree of obedience.

Step 2: Consideration: One day, a ten-year-old boy went to an ice cream shop, sat at a table and asked the waitress, "How much is an ice-cream cone?" She said, "seventy-five cents." The boy started counting the coins he had in his hand. Then he asked how much a small cup of ice-cream was. The waitress impatiently replied, "sixty-five cents." The boy said, "I will have the small ice-cream cup." He had his ice-cream, paid the bill and left. When the waitress came to pick up the empty plate, she was touched. Underneath were ten one-cent coins as tip. The little boy had consideration for the waitress before he ordered his ice-crearn. He showed sensitivity and caring. He thought of others before himself. If we all thought like the little boy, we would have a great place to live. Show consideration, courtesy, and politeness. Thoughtfulness shows a caring attitude.

Step 3: Think Win/Win: A man died and St. Peter asked him if he would like to go to heaven or hell. The man asked if he could see both before deciding. St. Peter took him to hell first and the man saw a big hall with a long table, lots of food on it and music playing. He also saw rows of people with pale, sad faces. They looked starved and there was no laughter. And he observed one more thing. Their hands were tied to four-foot forks and knives and they were trying to get the food from the center of the table to put into their mouths. But they couldn't. Then, he went to see heaven. There he saw a big hall with a long table, with lots of food on the table and music playing. He noticed rows of people on both sides of the table with their hands tied to four-foot forks and knives also. But he observed there was something different here. People were laughing and were well-fed and healthy-looking. He noticed that they were feeding one another across the table. The result was happiness, prosperity, enjoyment, and gratification because they were not thinking of themselves alone; they were thinking win/win. The same is true of our lives. When we serve our customers, our families, our employers and employees, we automatically win.

Step 4: Choose Your Words Carefully: A person who says what he likes usually ends up hearing what he doesn't like. Be tactful. Tact consists of choosing one's words carefully and knowing how far to go. It also means knowing what to say and what to leave unsaid. Talent without tact may not always be desirable. Words reflect attitude. Words can hurt feelings and destroy relationships. More people have been hurt by an improper choice of words than by any natural disaster. Choose what you say rather than say what you choose. That is the difference between wisdom and foolishness. Excessive talking does not mean communication. Talk less; say more. A fool speaks without thinking; a wise man thinks before speaking. Words spoken out of bitterness can cause irreparable damage. The way parents speak to their children in many instances shapes their children's destiny.

Step 5: Don't Criticize and Complain: When I talk of criticism I refer to negative criticism. Why should we not criticize? When a person is criticized, he becomes defensive. Does that mean we should never criticize, or can we give positive criticism? A critic is like a back-seat driver who drives the driver mad.

Positive Criticism what is constructive criticism? Criticize with a spirit of helpfulness rather than as a put-down. Offer solutions in your criticism. Criticize the behavior, not the person, because when we criticize the person, we hurt their self esteem. The right to criticize comes with the desire to help. As long as the act of criticizing does not give pleasure to the giver, it is okay. When giving criticism becomes a pleasure, it is time to stop.

Step 6: Smile and Be Kind: Cheerfulness flows from goodness. A smile can be fake or genuine. The key is to have a genuine one. It takes more muscles to frown than to smile. It is easier to smile than frown. It improves face value. A simile is contagious and is an inexpensive way to improve looks. A smiling face is always welcome. Who likes to be around a grouch? No one, except maybe a bigger grouch. A warm sincere smile shows through just like an insincere one.

Step 7: Put Positive Interpretation on Other People's Behavior: In the absence of sufficient facts, people instinctively put a negative interpretation on others' actions or inactions. Some people suffer from "paranoia"; they think the world is out to get them. That is not true. By starting on a positive note, we have a better chance of building a pleasing personality resulting in good relationships. For example, how often have we put through a call and not gotten a reply from the other party for two days and the first thought that comes to our mind is, "They never cared to return my call" or "They ignored me." That is negative. Maybe:

¨ they tried, but couldn't get through they left the message we didn't get

¨ they had an emergency

¨ they never got the message

There could be many reasons. It is worth giving the benefit of doubt to the other person and starting on a positive note.

Step 8: Be a Good Listener: Ask yourself these questions. How does it make you feel when you wanted somebody to listen to you and

- They did more talking than listening?
- They disagreed with the first thing you said.
- They interrupted you at every step.
- They were impatient and completed every sentence you started.
- They were physically present but mentally absent.
- They heard but didn't listen. You had to repeat the same thing three times because the other person wasn't listening.
- They came to conclusions unrelated to facts.
- They asked questions on unrelated topics.
- They were fidgety and distracted.
- They were obviously not listening or paying attention.

All these things show disinterest in the person or the topic and a total lack of courtesy.

Step 9: Be Enthusiastic: Enthusiasm and success go hand in hand, but enthusiasm comes first. Enthusiasm inspires confidence, raises morale, builds loyalty! and is priceless. Enthusiasm is contagious. You can feel enthusiasm by the way a person talks, walks or shakes hands. Enthusiasm is a habit that one can acquire and practice.

Step 10: Give Honest and Sincere Appreciation: The psychologist William James said, "One of the deepest desires of human beings is the desire to be appreciated. The feeling of being unwanted is hurtful." Expensive jewels are not real gifts; they are apologies for shortcomings. Many times we buy gifts for people to compensate for not spending enough time with them. Real gifts are when you give a part of yourself.

Sincere appreciation is one of the greatest gifts one can give to another person. It makes a person feel important. The desire to feel important is one of the greatest cravings in most human beings. It can be a great motivator. With these ten above mentioned traits one can build a positive personality.

Goal Setting

Goal setting involves establishing specific, measurable and time-targeted objectives.

Goal setting is a major component of personal development literature.

Effective goals should be tangible, specific, realistic and have a time targeted for completion. There must be realistic plans to achieve the intended goal. For example, setting a goal to go to Mars on a shoe string budget is not a realistic goal, while setting a goal to go to Hawaii as a backpacker is a possible goal with possible, realistic plans.

Work on the theory of goal-setting suggests that it's an effective tool for making progress by ensuring that participants in a group with a common goal are clearly aware of what is expected from them if an objective is to be achieved. On a personal level, setting goals is a process that allows people to specify then work towards their own objectives - most commonly with financial or career-based goals. However, some say that much of what is currently taught about goal setting is incomplete. Prominent speakers on goal setting such as Jim Rohn or Zig Ziglar have suggested that goal setting is more than writing something down, setting a date and working towards that end. In order to make the success or achievement a lasting value the person must become something different in the process. There are significant differences in how a person accomplishes a "be" goal (Character driven) versus a "Have" goal. (An accomplishment or a possession to obtain.)

Some people feel that one possible drawback of goal setting is that implicit learning may be inhibited. This is because goal setting may encourage simple focus on an outcome without openness to exploration, understanding or growth. "Goals provide a sense of direction and purpose" (Goldstein, 1993, p. 96). Locke et al. (1981) examined the behavioral effects of goal-setting, concluding that 90% of laboratory and field studies involving specific and challenging goals led to higher performance than easy or no goals. In business, goal setting has the advantages of encouraging participants to put in substantial effort; and, because every member has defined expectations set upon him or her (high role perception), little room is left for inadequate effort going unnoticed.

While some managers would believe it is sufficient to urge employees to 'do their best', Locke and Latham have a clear contradicting view on this. The authors state that people who are told to 'do their best' will not do so. 'Doing your best' has no external referent which implies that it is useless in eliciting specific behavior. To elicit some specific form of behavior from others, it is important that this person has a clear view of what is expected from him/her. A goal is thereby of vital importance because it facilitates an individual in focusing their efforts in a specified direction. In other words; goals canalize behavior (Cummings & Worley p. 368). However when goals are established at a management level and thereafter solely laid down, employee motivation with regard to achieving these goals is rather suppressed (Locke & Latham, 2002 p. 705). In order to increase motivation the employees not only need to be allowed to participate in the goal setting process but the goals have to be challenging as well (Cummings & Worley p. 369).

Managers cannot be constantly able to drive motivation and keep track of an employee's work on a continuous basis. Goals are therefore an important tool for managers since goals have the ability to function as a self-regulatory mechanism that acquires an employee a certain amount of guidance have distilled four mechanisms through which goal setting is able to affect individual performance:

1. Goals focus attention towards goal-relevant activities and away from goal-irrelevant activities.
2. Goals serve as an energizer; higher goals will induce greater effort while low goals induce lesser effort.
3. Goals affect persistence; constraints with regard to resources will affect work pace.
4. Goals activate cognitive knowledge and strategies which allows employees to cope with the situation at hand.

Through an understanding of the effect of goal setting on individual performance organizations are able to use goal setting to benefit organizational performance. Have therefore indicated three moderators which indicate the success of goal setting:

Goal Commitment

People will perform better when they are committed to achieve certain goals. Goal commitment is dependent of:

1. The importance of the expected outcomes of goal attainment and;
2. Self-efficacy—one's belief that they are able to achieve the goals;
3. Commitment to others—promises or engagements to others can strongly improve commitment.

Feedback

Keep track of performance to allow employees to see how effective they have been in attaining the goals. Without proper feedback channels it is impossible to adapt or adjust to the required behavior.

Task Complexity

More difficult goals require more cognitive strategies and well developed skills. The more difficult the tasks ahead, a smaller group of people will possess the necessary skills and strategies. From an organizational perspective it is thereby more difficult to successfully attain more difficult goals since resources become more scarce.

Employee Motivation

The more employees are motivated, the more they are stimulated and interested in accepting goals.

Macro-economical Characteristics

The position of the economy in the conjecture puts pressure or simply relieves the organization. This means that some goals are easier set in specific macro-economical surroundings. Depression is for instance the least successful conjectural phase for goal setting.

These success factors are not to be seen independently. For example the expected outcomes of goals are positively influenced when employees are involved in the goal setting process. Not only does participation increase commitment in attaining the goals that are set, participation influences self-efficacy as well. In addition to this feedback is necessary to monitor one's progress. When this is left aside, an employee might think (s) he is not making enough progress. This can reduce self-efficacy and thereby harm the performance outcomes in the long run.

Setting Good Goals

Whether this is your first experience with setting goals or you've been setting them all of your life, here are some helpful suggestions and ideas. Experienced goal-setters will notice that myGoals.com does a few things differently from traditional paper-based systems, owing to the power and flexibility of the Internet.

What Makes a Good Goal?

Traditional goal-setting wisdom has taught us that a good goal must be (*a*) written, (*b*) challenging, (*c*) believable, (*d*) specific, (*e*) measurable, and (*f*) have a specific deadline. Unfortunately, it's not too difficult to think of an example that directly challenges any of the above goal-setting criteria. For instance, the goal "to live a more spiritual life" may be a valuable, meaningful goal for many, but it's hardly measurable and assigning a deadline makes little sense for a permanent alteration of lifestyle. This traditional checklist of things that "make a good goal" is largely a product of old technology: pen and paper. The old-school of goal-setting suggested that people write down goals on a small slip of paper and keep it in their wallet or purse. Suffice to say that slips of paper rapidly dissolve into lint. Today we have email.

So what makes a good goal? All of the above criteria are still good components of most goals. However, they are not necessarily all required when using myGoals.com. For our purposes, a good goal is one that is worthy of individual pursuit. And that is so highly subjective, far be it from us to define what your worthy pursuit is. A different question is, "What makes a good Goal plan?" On this, our position is precise: A good Goal plan is one that when followed, offers a reasonably high probability of success, given sufficient time. Let's take each of the traditional point's one-at-a-time:

- *Must all goals be written?* It's important to record your goals, whether you enter them into myGoals.com or physically write them down on paper. The problem with the paper method is that hand-written goals are difficult to update and manage, and of course, hand-written goals provide none of the additional features that are made possible by the Web.
- *Must all goals be believable?* You must believe that it is at least possible for you to achieve the goal or you will not be motivated to try. More importantly, it is *you* who must believe, not others (see what to do about naysayer). Also, just because you should believe that the goal is *possible* does not mean that you must expect it to be *easy* or even probable. Indeed,

some argue that completion of only the most difficult goals will have enduring value to you. Similarly, some of history's greatest moments was the result of people attempting the "impossible," such as flying or putting a man on the moon? See more about setting "realistic" goals.

- *Must all goals be challenging?* No. We recommend setting at least one easy goal and at least one challenging goal. You could have several of each but you should limit the number of challenging goals or tasks coming due at any one time to avoid becoming overwhelmed or frustrated. The easy goals build good habits of follow-through and reward you with quick gratification. The challenging goals force you to grow. A mix of the two is ideal.
- *Must all goals be measurable and specific?* Your goals should be measurable and specific enough for you to know unambiguously whether they have been completed yet or not. However, to save space on the computer screen, abbreviated goal titles such as "to reduce my stress" might be more convenient than titles such as "to reduce my stress by practicing yoga three nights a week and lowering my blood pressure by 10 points." Instead, make individual *tasks* in myGoals.com measurable and specific as much as possible, even if the details must be written in the task's "notes" area.
- *Must all goals have deadlines?* Here's the big shocker: Goals no longer have to have a deadline! Technology has allowed us to expand the definition of what a goal can be to include a *direction, commitment, or lifestyle enhancement* as opposed to a mere end-point. The technology utilized in myGoals.com allows a new and completely revolutionary look at the need for a goal to have a deadline. We offer a new type of goal called an "on-going" goal, that is sustained over time,

managed, and tracked, but by design, never-ending. Why, for instance, would you want to end a goal, "to keep myself in excellent physical condition" or "to be an honest and trustworthy person"? Such goals should have no end-date, and now they don't have to. This concept may sound revolutionary to long-time power goal-setters. It *is* revolutionary. We invite you to try it.

Should my goals be short-term or long-term? We recommend that you always have *at least one short-term and one long-term goal* at any given time. Short-term goals are usually simpler and easier than long-term. Setting them helps assure that you'll have frequent victories, building a strong track record and momentum with each one you complete.

Long-term goals (two years or longer) keep you headed in the right direction and can provide a sense of greater purpose, not to mention something exciting to work toward.

It's okay to change goals as you go. With long-term goals, it's important not to focus on the goal so much that you lose sight of the underlying reason you set the goal in the first place. The world changes and so can you. While follow-through and persistence are among the most important traits related to long-term accomplishment, so is the ability to re-assess along the way. So long as you are honest with yourself, it's okay to change your mind, change goals mid-stream, shelve one for a later day, or cancel one altogether. Again, the trick is to be honest with yourself, and not change your mind so frequently that you never accomplish anything. (See also "What if my goals change?")

Should my goals be lofty or practical? Only you can decide what is "lofty" or "practical" and how many goals of either flavor you'd like to set. Indeed, one person's lofty might be another's practical, and vice-versa. This service is here to help you accomplish anything you set out to do, from painting the house to reforming public education. And while we're always thrilled to hear success stories from our users who've done newsworthy and inspiring things, we also know that these can't be done without also taking care of the simpler items on life's to-do list.

But assuming you've covered your bases and been mindful of the balanced whole, and if you've got the energy and passion to apply to something beyond the ordinary, then-by all means-reach for the stars! Along these same lines, be sure to also see:

- Must all goals be challenging?
- Must all goals be believable?
- How do I know if a goal is realistic?

With lofty goals, pay extra attention to whom you're willing to discuss your goals with, particularly when you first begin and have no demonstrable milestones achieved. The old adage, "show, don't tell," exists because naysayer are quick to label lofty goal-setters as fools or dreamers, and deeds shut them up faster than promises. Your personal support group of family and friends (at least, those whom you trust to be supportive) is an exception. Use them as a resource whenever appropriate. For more on dealing with naysayer, "Should I keep my goals private?" How do I know if a goal is realistic? A goal is realistic if you stand reasonably good odds of accomplishing it, given enough time and effort-and indeed, mountains can be moved if given enough time and effort. "Good odds" is a subjective measure, but one that you have most control over when success or failure depends on what *you* do, as opposed to what other people do or random events (such as goals "to become an astronaut" or "to win the lottery").

The majority of the goals you set should be very realistic or you risk becoming frustrated if you do not accomplish any of them. However, there is nothing wrong with attempting things that defy the odds or that you expect to be extremely difficult. Such goals require courage, defined here as "attempting something even though you might not succeed." Almost any goal, no matter how difficult, can be made easier by breaking it down into several smaller goals, to be tackled one at a time. The completion of so-called "baby steps" is one of the best ways to build confidence, momentum, and a track record of performance. And finally, when you create or update a Goal plan, ask yourself, "Will completing these steps lead to completion of the goal?" If not, then modify the obstacles, tasks, or due dates until a viable plan exists. How many goals should I have at the same time? You can *set* many goals without worrying about spreading yourself too thin because we make a distinction between *"setting"* a goal and *"working on"* a goal. These are not necessarily the same thing because, with myGoals.com, you can set goals that do not begin until some future date, even years from now. The idea is that you should be thinking of goals you'd like to shoot for in the future even if you are focused on other things going on in your life right now.

- *How many goals can I set?* A goal is "set" when you create a Goal plan, even if you only create a partial plan with the intention of filling in the details later. In fact, you might just write down the name of the goal, for no other reason than to remind you that's it's something you'd like to do later. (You can always edit any of your Goal plans at any later date.)
- *How many goals can I "work on" at the same time?* Here, "working on" refers to goals that have begun-meaning the start date you entered has passed. For instance, you might have a goal to run a marathon next year but you might not intend to begin working on this goal (training, etc.) until six months from now. So you would set the start date to occur in six months. So for six months, nothing happens, but you'll see the goal every time you visit, thereby being reminded that this goal exists on the horizon. Only after the start date elapses would the Goal plan

become active, sending you task reminders related to that goal. While there is no technical limit to how many goals you can be working on simultaneously at myGoals.com, it would be easy to overload yourself with too many goals-in-progress. You only have so many hours in a day and so many things you can adequately address at a given time.

We therefore suggest you limit the number of goals you're working on to some manageable number, which for most people will be *somewhere between 5 and 10 goals*, depending on a few common-sense factors:

How focused can you be? If you've got a lot going on in your life right now, little spare time, or if you really need to focus intently on a small number of important things, then don't attempt to take on too many goals at once. It's better to keep your number of goals down to a manageable amount so that you can actually accomplish a few of them now and then (which are much more fun than having many goals that rarely ever get accomplished). With that said, also be mindful of the importance of balance. Even if you are much focused on one important goal, don't forget the other important things such as your health or personal relationships.

- *How difficult are your goals?* Some people use myGoals.com for goals as simple as "To clean my desk." Others use it for goals like "To sell my company." (We suggest you use it for both challenging and easy goals, *at least one of each.*) The simpler your goals are, the more goals you can be working on simultaneously without causing problems. You might be able to handle twenty "clean my desk"-type goals simultaneously but only one or two "sell my company"-type goals.
- *Are your goals short-term or long-term?* We also recommend using myGoals.com for both short-term

and long-term goals (*at least one of each*). Keep in mind however, that the more short-term goals you have, the more tasks you're likely to have coming due soon. To avoid having too many tasks come due at the same time, you might want to have fewer goals if they are mostly short-term goals.

- What if my goals conflict with each other? Almost all goals require some of your resources: time, money, effort, attention, and so on. Because these resources are limited, goals can often appear to be at odds with one another-working on one can mean slipping on the other. Good management of your goals *as a group* is important for avoiding frustration:
- *Stay focused.* Don't set too many goals to come due at the same time. A large number of goals (7+) are okay if the goals are small or simple (such as a goal to shampoo the carpet) but be realistic and don't expect to build a business *while* getting a law degree *while* training for a triathlon *while* raising a family.
- *Always have at least one simple goal and one difficult goal at any given time.* The simple goals motivate you as you accomplish them rapidly. The difficult goals keep you challenged and growing.
- *Always have at least one short-term and one long-term goal at any given time.* As with simple goals, short-term goals help assure that you'll have frequent victories. Long-term goals (two years or longer) keep you headed in the right direction.
- *Prioritize but be flexible.* Decide which of your goals (and tasks) are most important and assign your due dates accordingly. Be willing to change due dates or even put a goal on hold for a while if necessary.
- *Spread out your due dates.* Avoid setting a large number of difficult goals with tasks due at the same time.

- *Look for ways to combine goals and tasks.* For instance, if you have a goal to take a vacation and a goal to get better at photography, consider taking a travel photography class that spends a week in the wilderness snapping picks.
- *Most of all, strive for balance.* Make sure to set goals (whether easy or hard) across different areas of your life: health, finance, family, relations, learning, experiencing, career, etc. For instance, don't set ten career goals but then neglect your health, friends, and family.

Success Strategies

1. Know what success is: If you don't know what success is (for you), how can you possibly create it? Success is different things for different people and one person's success (a pregnancy for example) might be another person's catastrophe. That's because success (or failure) is not so much about the situation, circumstance, event or outcome as it is about what that "thing" means to the person in the middle of it. In order to create success, you must first define it – and far too many people haven't. Be very clear about what you want and don't want for your life. Clarity produces excitement. Excitement produces momentum. Momentum produces behavioural change. Behavioural change produces different results and eventually, the internal vision becomes an external reality.

2. Get comfortable being uncomfortable: Some people will live a life of second-best, of compromise and of under-achievement simply because they are (1) controlled by fear (2) always looking for the magic pill or shortcut and (3) not prepared to do the tough stuff. People who always take the easy option are destined for mediocrity. Constantly avoiding the discomfort means constantly avoiding the lessons and the personal growth. Pain is a great teacher. Not always what we want, but sometimes what we need.

3. Seek to be righteous, not right: The need to be "right" speaks of arrogance, insecurity, ego and stupidity. It's also synonymous with failure. The person who constantly needs to be right will miss out on much of what life has to teach him and alienate him from others. Arrogance repels, humility attracts.

4. Seek respect, not popularity: It's been said that our nature is "who we are" and our reputation is who people think we are. When the two are synonymous, we're usually on the right path.

5. Embrace mess: To embrace mess is to embrace life because life is messy, unpredictable, unfair, uncertain, lumpy and bumpy. So get used to a little chaos. Embrace it even. While others succumb to the messiness and unpredictability of the human experience, make a conscious choice to be the calm in the chaos.

6. Don't become your parents: Or your boss. Or anyone but you. The enormity of conformity is a problem for the want to-be success story. Sure, your parents are great and by all means respect them, love them and learn from them, but please don't become them; that's just plain ugly and a little bit tragic. Listen to, and learn from other people, but think, act and decide for yourself. And no, you don't need anyone's approval or permission; you're big now. It's okay.

7. Use more of what you already have: Imagine what you could achieve if you took all the knowledge, intelligence, opportunities, time, skill and talent that you currently have and absolutely milked it. What if you already have more than enough talent to become wildly successful? Well, you do. There go the excuses. And that voice that's telling (some of) you right now that you don't have what it takes to become successful, that's called fear. Not logic, fear. Not reality, fear. Unless of course, you allow that to become your reality. Bc mindful that the voice in your head (the very loud, annoying and persistent one) is rarely a reflection of your potential and mostly a manifestation of your insecurity. And no, you're not alone in your self-doubt; it's a universal condition. Many people fail, not because they don't have what it takes, but because they don't use what they already have. Successful people typically don't have more innate potential, luck, time or opportunity than the next person, but they consistently find a way to use much more of what they have at their disposal. While the majority are rationalising their lack of decision making and action taking, these guys are finding a way to get the job done. The question is not "how much ability do you have, but how much will you use?"

8. Be an innovator, not an imitator: Not too many sheep succeed. Baaah. Sometimes it's a good idea to build your own team rather than join someone else's. Don't let your fear stand in the way of your potential to create, innovate or lead. When I set up Australia's first commercial personal training centre, most people told me it wouldn't work. Glad I didn't listen.

9. Do what most won't: If you want to achieve what most people won't (happiness, joy, calm, wealth, optimal health, balance) then don't do what they do. If you want to be like the majority, then do what they do. Producing different results comes from doing different things. Simple really. And effective. Most people won't persevere, won't finish what they start, won't find the good, won't do what it takes, won't question their long-held beliefs, won't be solution-focused, won't do what scares them and won't "be the change" they want to see in their world. Choose to be different.

10. Be like water. Powerful. Gentle. Adaptable. Ever-changing: Being static in a dynamic world—like the one you and I inhabit—is a recipe for disaster. If you can't adapt, you can't succeed. Our practical, three dimensional realities, and everything in it, is in a constant state of transition, while some of us are in a constant state of "same". Statues don't succeed, they just get crapped on.

Team Building

Team building refers to a wide range of activities, usually in a business context, for improving team performance. Team building is pursued via a variety of practices, and can range from simple bonding exercises to complex simulations and multi-day team building retreats designed to develop a team (including group assessment and group-dynamic games), usually falling somewhere in between. It generally sits within the theory and practice of organizational development, but can also be applied to sports teams, school groups, and other contexts. Team building is not to be confused with "team recreation" that consists of activities for teams that are strictly recreational. Teambuilding is an important factor in any environment, its focus is to specialize in bringing out the best in a team to ensure self development, positive communication, leadership skills and the ability to work closely together as a team to problem solve.

Work environments tend to focus on individuals and personal goals, with reward & recognition singling out the achievements of individual employees. "How to create effective teams is a challenge in every organization" Team building can also refer to the process of selecting or creating a team from scratch.

History of Team Building

- Sigmund Freud (1921, 1960) discussed a theory of group dynamic termed identification with the leader which is the foundation of group formation.
- McDougall (1920) tends to be credited for being the first team builder and suggested five different conditions needed for a high functioning group.
- Taylor (1947) discovered how group norms impact performance.
- Lewin (1945) founded the Center for Research in Group Dynamics and laboratory studies were conducted.

- World War II brought increased research/attention to team performance.
- During the 1970s theory and methodologies were available for large-scale team building. However, work culture tended to not be supportive of teamwork and rather rewarded individual behavior.
- From the early 1980s until 1990, the United States began to rethink business and viewed teams differently given the economics with inflation rising and significant international debt. Team-based reward systems were implemented.
- The years 1990 to present are considered the era of high-performance teams. Consulting firms developed methods and tools to help organizations with the transition to team-based organization.
- Ben Aldham (1979) developed a mathematical rule to explain the improvement in team cohesiveness with relation to team alcohol consumption. It was published in 2003 as the "Rule of Ben".

What does a Team-Building Consultant do?

A team-building consultant is responsible for each component of a team building intervention. A team-building consultant will likely interact with the team once, or for a limited number of times. During this relationship, the consultant will actively work to assess the team, make recommendations, and provide activities (exercises that compose a team building intervention) for the team. These responsibilities usually require a team-building consultant to write a proposal after his or her evaluation of the organization and the team, indicating how he or she would go about improving the team's performance. Once the organization and consultant determine which recommendations to utilize (if not all), the consultant is then responsible for providing a useful intervention that will transfer back into the organizational setting. This responsibility usually requires the consultant to create a detailed plan of events, while allowing for flexibility. After the intervention has been employed, the consultant will typically evaluate the team-building program and communicate the results to the organization. Otherwise!!

Things a Team-Building Consultant Might Ask

What does your organization want to get out of the exercise? The organization should make their goals clear to a team-building consultant or facilitator. This will allow the consultant to more effectively work with the organization to find the best exercises that fit their needs.

What are the needs of the current team? Sometimes an organization will not know exactly what is wrong with a team. The team itself may have some clear ideas about what they need to improve on. Again, a consultant or facilitator will be able to assist the team better if they are able to get this kind of information. With this information, they can tailor the team building and individual exercises to best help the team.

What is the general age of the participants within the team? Some team building exercises are designed for younger groups. These exercises are not appropriate for older groups and could cause the organization and the team members to think that team building is a waste of time. In addition, some exercises are simply beyond some individuals physical capabilities. It is important to make exercises all-inclusive, so that all individuals within the teams can participate.

Reasons for Team Building

Reasons for Team Building include:

- Improving communication
- Making the workplace more enjoyable
- Motivating a team
- Getting to know each other

- Getting everyone "onto the same page", including goal setting
- Teaching the team self-regulation strategies
- Helping participants to learn more about themselves (strengths and weaknesses)
- Identifying and utilizing the strengths of team members
- Improving team productivity
- Practicing effective collaboration with team members

What are Team Building Exercises and what is their Purpose?

Team building exercises consist of a variety of tasks designed to develop group members and their ability to work together effectively. There are many types of team building activities that range from kids games to games that involve novel complex tasks and are designed for specific needs. There are also more complex team building exercises that are composed of multiple exercises such as ropes courses, corporate drumming and exercises that last over several days. The purpose of team building exercises is to assist teams in becoming cohesive units of individuals that can effectively work together to complete tasks.

Who can Benefit from Team Building Exercises?

Team building exercises are useful for all kinds of teams. Some exercises are designed for smaller teams, some for larger teams. Some are designed for new teams, others to focus on specific areas of an established team to be worked on. In addition to this, team building exercises also are for different age groups. In addition to this, some team building exercises are intended primarily for a specific age group. It is possible that some team building activities designed for younger teams being misused with more mature groups has contributed to the negative stigma frequently associated with team building exercises.

TYPES OF TEAM BUILDING EXERCISES

Communication Exercise

This type of team building exercise is exactly what it sounds like. Communications exercises are problem solving activities that are geared towards improving communication skills. The issues teams encounter in these exercises are solved by communicating effectively with each other.

Goal: Create an activity which highlights the importance of good communication in team performance and/or potential problems with communication.

Problem Solving/Decision Making Exercise

Problem Solving/Decision making exercises focus specifically on groups working together to solve difficult problems or make complex decisions. These exercises are some of the most common as they appear to have the most direct link to what employers want their teams to be able to do.

Goal: Give team a problem in which the solution is not easily apparent or requires the team to come up with a creative solution

Planning/Adaptability Exercise

These exercises focus on aspects of planning and being adaptable to change. These are important things for teams to be able to do when they are assigned complex tasks or decisions.

Goal: Show the importance of planning before implementing a solution

Trust Exercise

A trust exercise involves engaging team members in a way that will induce trust between them. They are sometimes difficult exercises to implement as there are varying degrees of trust between individuals and varying degrees of individual comfort trusting others in general.

Goal: Create trust between team members

Methods for Team Building

Team building events often take participants out of their regular work context, and use the new context as an enabler of change and development - allowing team participants to get to learn more about each other in a new (nonwork) context.

COMPONENTS OF A TEAM BUILDING EXERCISE

Part 1: Instructions

This part of a team-building exercise involves introducing the participants to the instructions for the exercise.

Part 2: Activity

This part of the team-building exercise is the exercise itself. This is when participants utilize the instructions and begin to participate in the actual activity.

Part 3: Debriefing

This is the most important part of a team building exercise. The facilitator will close the exercise with a review of the purpose for the exercise and how the team accomplished it. For the debriefing portion of the team building exercise using open ended questions is a tool that a team building facilitator uses to bring participants to examine what was learned.

These questions have no right and wrong answer they are meant to trigger thought and insight in the team members. These questions can be used for front loading - setting up the thoughts prior to the beginning of a team building activity. These questions can also be used following an activity to reflect on the individual experience, team experience and actions plans for behavioral change within the team. Below are examples of open ended questions that get results and inspire team work.

What was the first clue that the situation was not going well? How did the chaos stop? What had to happen before you could start working towards a solution? What type of solution were you, as small teams, striving for? What are some real examples from your work lives that mirror this activity? As a team initiative, which elements of high performing teams were evident and which elements needed more emphasis? Clarity of purpose and clarity of roles are essential for team performance. How did these two factors influence performance? What similarities do you see between this and the workplace? Is there anything we want to focus our attention on in future initiatives?

How did you use your planning time? Was everyone incorporated into the planning, if not why? Those of you who did not feel part of the team what stopped you from pushing your way in? Was a common language created? How is this like work? How can we implement our learning into the team? What strategies did the group develop to implement an effective solution? What was the consequence of change during the activity? What strategies did the group develop to adjust to change? What recommendations does the group have for managing change at work based on the experience? How did this activity build trust? What changes have you noticed since you finished the stages? How did you overcome any anxieties? How well did you coach your partner? Using an open ended question will raise ideas and create solutions that teams never thought possible. The methods of doing this vary widely, including

- simple social activities—to encourage team members to spend time together.
- group bonding sessions—company sponsored fun activities to get to know team members (sometimes intending also to inspire creativity).

- personal development activities – individual programs given to groups (sometimes physically challenging).
- team development activities – group-dynamic games designed to help individuals discover how they approach a problem, how the team works together, and discover better methods.
- psychological analysis of team roles, and training in how to work better together.

Team interaction involves "soft" interpersonal skills including communication, negotiation, leadership, and motivation – in contrast to technical skills directly involved with the job at hand. Depending on the type of team building, the novel tasks can encourage or specifically teach interpersonal team skills to increase team performance.

Models of Team Behavior

Team building generally sits within the theory and practice of organizational development. The related field of *team management* refers to techniques, processes and tools for organizing and coordinating a team towards a common goal – as well as the inhibitors to teamwork and ways to remove, mitigate or overcome them.

- The forming-storming-norming-performing model posits four stages of new team development to reach high performance. Some team activities are designed to speed up (or improve) this process in the safe team development environment.
- Belbin Team Types can be assessed to gain insight into an individual's natural behavioral tendencies in a team context, and can be used to create and develop better functioning teams.

TEAM MEMBER QUALITIES

Emotional Stability

- Adjustment
- Self-esteem

Extraversion

- Dominance
- Affiliation
- Social Perceptiveness
- Expressivity

Openness

- Flexibility

Agreeableness

- Trust
- Cooperation

In breaking down these dimensions, it was generalized that past research has been consistent when it mentions that emotional stability, extraversion, openness, agreeableness, and conscientiousness are all related to team effectiveness. Within extraversion, dominance was found to be a negative attribute in team members where they are not working independently and not collaborating with others. Adjustment and flexibility were noted to be important facets for team members to have where adjustment to situations is needed. Clearly for teams to be successful there has to be a balance between the personality dimensions. This provides well-roundedness for a person to bring to a team.

Organizational Development

In the organizational development context, a team may embark on a process of self-assessment to gauge its effectiveness and improve its performance. To assess itself, a team seeks feedback from group members to find out both its current strengths and weakness..

To improve its current performance, feedback from the team assessment can be used to identify gaps between the desired state and the current state, and to design a gap-closure strategy. Team development can be the greater term containing this assessment and improvement actions, or as a component of organizational development.

Building a New Team

The process for creating a new team is different from developing an existing team.

The following table gives us an understanding for the dimensions of the new task as a manager in the new team environment.

Old Environment	New Environment
Person followed orders.	Person comes up with initiatives.
Group depended on manager.	Group has considerable authority to chart its own steps.
Group was a team because people conformed to direction set by manager. No one rocked the boat.	Group is a team because people learn to collaborate in the face of their emerging right to think for themselves. People rock the boat and work together.
People cooperated by suppressing their thoughts and feelings. They wanted to get along.	People cooperate by using their thoughts and feelings. They link up through direct talk.

Topchik Identifies 10 Steps for Building a New Project Team

Get upper-management support

1. Define the purpose of your team
2. Identify time frames
3. Select team members
4. Classify team-member openings
5. Share the overall purpose
6. Decide team name

7. Create the team mission statement and goals
8. Determine core team issues
9. Establish team norms

Self-Managed Work Teams

Self-managing work teams (SMWTs) have been rising in popularity since the beginning of the 1990s. These team members are responsible for themselves. Although more organizations are implementing SMWTs, employees have been resisting them. Three variables at the individual-level are potential reasons for resistance to SMWTs. These variables include trust, cultural values and low tolerance for change.

Managers should implement SMWTs with procedural and distributive justice. Also, managers should address concerns regarding trust, and accountability. They should provide clarity regarding who is responsible for what and how the employees' careers and opportunities for development will be affected. Managers should work to encourage employees having a positive organizational outlook.

Team Building

Team building" (or "'teambuilding'") refers to the process of establishing and developing a greater sense of collaboration and trust between team members. Interactive exercises, team assessments, and group discussions enable groups to cultivate this greater sense of teamwork.

Characteristics of Good Team Building

- High level of interdependence among team members
- Team leader has good people skills and is committed to team approach
- Each team member is willing to contribute
- Team develops a relaxed climate for communication
- Team members develop a mutual trust

- Team and individuals are prepared to take risks
- Team is clear about goals and establishes targets
- Team member roles are defined
- Team members know how to examine team and individual errors without personal attacks
- Team has capacity to create new ideas
- Each team member knows he can influence the team agenda

Team Effectiveness

When evaluating how well team members are working together, the following statements can be used as a guide:

Team goals are developed through a group process of team interaction and agreement in which each team member is willing to work toward achieving these goals.

Participation is actively shown by all team members and roles are shared to facilitate the accomplishment of tasks and feelings of group togetherness.

Feedback is asked for by members and freely given as a way of evaluating the team's performance and clarifying both feelings and interests of the team members. When feedback is given it is done with a desire to help the other person.

Team decision making involves a process that encourages active participation by all members.

Leadership is distributed and shared among team members and individuals willingly contribute their resources as needed.

Problem solving, discussing team issues, and critiquing team effectiveness are encouraged by all team members.

Conflict is not suppressed. Team members are allowed to express negative feelings and confrontation within the team which is managed and dealt with by team members. Dealing with and managing conflict is seen as a way to improve team performance.

Team member resources, talents, skills, knowledge, and experiences are fully identified, recognized, and used whenever appropriate.

Risk taking and creativity are encouraged. When mistakes are made, they are treated as a source of learning rather than reasons for punishment. After evaluating team performance against the above guidelines, determine those areas in which the team members need to improve and develop a strategy for doing so.

Inside-Out: The Change Starts from Within

While working on his doctorate in the 1970's, Stephen R. Covey reviewed 200 years of literature on success. He noticed that since the 1920's, success writings have focused on solutions to specific problems. In some cases such tactical advice may have been effective, but only for immediate issues and not for the long-term, underlying ones. The success literature of the last half of the 20th century largely attributed success to personality traits, skills, techniques, maintaining a positive attitude, etc. This philosophy can be referred to as the *Personality Ethic.*

However, during the 150 years or so that preceded that period, the literature on success was more character oriented. It emphasized the deeper principles and foundations of success. This philosophy is known as the *Character Ethic,* under which success is attributed more to underlying characteristics such as integrity, courage, justice, patience, etc.

The elements of the Character Ethic are primary traits while those of the Personality Ethic are secondary. While secondary traits may help one to play the game to succeed in some specific circumstances, for long-term success both are necessary. One's character is what is most visible in long-term relationships. Ralph Waldo Emerson once said, "What you are shouts so loudly in my ears I cannot hear what you say."

To illustrate the difference between primary and secondary traits, Covey offers the following example. Suppose you are in Chicago and are using a map to find a particular destination in the city. You may have excellent secondary skills in map reading and navigation, but will never find your destination if you are using a map of Detroit. In this example, getting the right map is a necessary primary element before your secondary skills can be used effectively.

The problem with relying on the Personality Ethic is that unless the basic underlying paradigms are right, simply changing outward behavior is not effective. We see the world based on our perspective, which can have a dramatic impact on the way we perceive things. For example, many experiments have been conducted in which two groups of people are shown two different drawings. One group is shown, for instance, a drawing of a young, beautiful woman and the other group is shown a drawing of an old, frail woman. After the initial exposure to the pictures, both groups are shown one picture of a more abstract drawing. This drawing actually contains the elements of both the young and the old woman. Almost invariably, everybody in the group that was first shown the young woman sees a young woman in the abstract drawing, and those who were shown the old woman see an old woman. Each group was convinced that it had objectively evaluated the drawing. The point is that we see things not as they are, but as we are conditioned to see them. Once we understand the importance of our past conditioning, we can experience a paradigm shift in the way we see things. To make large changes in our lives, we must work on the basic paradigms through which we see the world.

The Character Ethic assumes that there are some absolute principles that exist in all human beings. Some examples of such principles are fairness, honesty, integrity, human dignity, quality, potential, and growth. Principles contrast with practices in that practices are for specific situations whereas principles have universal application.

The *Seven Habits of Highly Effective People* presents an "inside-out" approach to effectiveness that is centered on principles and character. Inside-out means that the change starts within oneself. For many people, this approach represents a paradigm shift away from the Personality Ethic and toward the Character Ethic.

The Seven Habits—An Overview

Our character is a collection of our habits, and habits have a powerful role in our lives. Habits consist of knowledge, skill, and desire. Knowledge allows us to know what to do, skill gives us the ability to know how to do it, and desire is the motivation to do it.

The Seven Habits move us through the following stages:

1. *Dependence:* the paradigm under which we are born, relying upon others to take care of us.
2. *Independence:* the paradigm under which we can make our own decisions and take care of ourselves.
3. *Interdependence:* the paradigm under which we cooperate to achieve something that cannot be achieved independently.

Much of the success literature today tends to value independence, encouraging people to become liberated and do their own thing. The reality is that we are interdependent, and the independent model is not optimal for use in an interdependent environment that requires leaders and team players.

To make the choice to become interdependent, one first must be independent, since dependent people have not yet developed the character for interdependence. Therefore, the first three habits focus on self-mastery that is, achieving the private victories required to move from dependence to independence. Finally, the seventh habit is one of renewal and continual improvement, that is, of building one's personal production capability. To be effective, one must find the proper balance between actually producing and improving one's capability to produce. Covey illustrates this point with the fable of the goose and the golden egg.

In the fable, a poor farmer's goose began laying a solid gold egg every day, and the farmer soon became rich. He also became greedy and figured that the goose must have many golden eggs within her. In order to obtain all of the eggs immediately, he killed the goose. Upon cutting it open he discovered that it was not full of golden eggs. The lesson is that if one attempts to maximize immediate production with no regard to the production capability, the capability will be lost. Effectiveness is a function of both production and the capacity to produce.

The need for balance between production and production capability applies to physical, financial, and human assets. For example, in an organization the person in charge of a particular machine may increase the machine's immediate production by postponing scheduled maintenance. As a result of the increased output, this person may be rewarded with a promotion. However, the increased immediate output comes at the expense of future production since more maintenance will have to be performed on the machine later. The person who inherits the mess may even be blamed for the inevitable downtime and high maintenance expense. Customer loyalty also is an asset to which the production and production capability balance applies. A restaurant may have a reputation for serving great food, but the owner may decide to cut costs and lower the quality of the food. Immediately, profits will soar, but soon the restaurant's reputation will be tarnished, the customer's trust will be lost, and profits will decline.

This does not mean that only production capacity is important. If one builds capacity but never uses it, there will be no production. There is a balance between building production capacity and actually producing. Finding the right tradeoff is central to one's effectiveness. The above has been an introduction and overview of the 7 Habits. The following introduces the first habit in Covey's framework.

FROM DEPENDENCE TO INDEPENDENCE

Habit 1: Be Proactive

A unique ability that sets humans apart from animals is self-awareness and the ability to choose how we respond to any stimulus. While conditioning can have a strong impact on our lives, we are not determined by it. There are three widely accepted theories of determinism: genetic, psychic, and environmental. Genetic determinism says that our nature is coded into our DNA, and that our personality traits are inherited from our grandparents. Psychic determinism says that our upbringing determines our personal tendencies, and that emotional pain that we felt at a young age is remembered and affects the way we behave today. Environmental determinism states that factors in our present environment are responsible for our situation, such as relatives, the national economy, etc. These theories of determinism each assume a model in which the stimulus determines the response.

Viktor Frankl was a Jewish psychiatrist who survived the death camps of Nazi Germany. While in the death camps, Frankl realized that he alone had the power to determine his response to the horror of the situation. He exercised the only freedom he had in that environment by envisioning himself teaching students after his release. He became an inspiration for others around him. He realized that in the middle of the stimulus-response model, humans have the freedom to choose.

Animals do not have this independent will. They respond to a stimulus like a computer responds to its program. They are not aware of their programming and do not have the ability to change it. The model of determinism was developed based on experiments with animals and neurotic people. Such a model neglects our ability to choose how we will respond to stimuli.

We can choose to be reactive to our environment. For example, if the weather is good, we will be happy. If the weather is bad, we will be unhappy. If people treat us well, we will feel well; if they don't, we will feel bad and become defensive. We also can choose to be proactive and not let our situation determine how we will feel. Reactive behavior can be a self-fulfilling prophecy. By accepting that there is nothing we can do about our situation, we in fact become passive and do nothing. The first habit of highly effective people is *proactively*. Proactive people are driven by values that are independent of the weather or how people treat them. Gandhi said, "They cannot take away our self respect if we do not give it to them." Our response to what happened to us affects us more than what actually happened. We can choose to use difficult situations to build our character and develop the ability to better handle such situations in the future.

Proactive people use their resourcefulness and initiative to find solutions rather than just reporting problems and waiting for other people to solve them. Being proactive means assessing the situation and developing a positive response for it. Organizations can be proactive rather than be at the mercy of their environment. For example, a company operating in an industry that is experiencing a downturn can develop a plan to cut costs and actually use the downturn to increase market share. Once we decide to be proactive, exactly where we focus our efforts becomes important. There are many concerns in our lives, but we do not always have control over them. One can draw a circle that represents areas of concern, and a smaller circle within the first that represents areas of control. Proactive people focus their efforts on the things over which they have influence, and in the process often expand their area of influence. Reactive people often focus their efforts on areas of concern over which they have no control. Their complaining and negative energy tend to shrink their circle of influence.

In our area of concern, we may have direct control, indirect control, or no control at all. We have direct control over problems caused by our own behavior. We can solve these problems by changing our habits. We have indirect control over problems related to other people's behavior. We can solve these problems by using various methods of human influence, such as empathy, confrontation, example, and persuasion. Many people have only a few basic methods such as fight or flight. For problems over which we have no control, first we must recognize that we have no control, and then gracefully accept that fact and make the best of the situation.

SUMMARY OF THE HABITS

Habit 1: Be Proactive

Change starts from within, and highly effective people make the decision to improve their lives through the things that they can influence rather than by simply reacting to external. Your life doesn't just "happen." Whether you know it or not, it is carefully designed by you. The choices, after all, are yours. You choose happiness. you choose sadness. you choose decisiveness. You choose ambivalence. You choose success. You choose failure. You choose courage. You choose fear. Just remember that every moment, every situation, provides a new choice. And in doing so, it gives you a perfect opportunity to do things differently to produce more positive results.

Be Proactive is about taking responsibility for your life. You can't keep blaming everything on your parents or grandparents. Proactive people recognize that they are "response-able." They don't blame genetics, circumstances, conditions, or conditioning for their behavior. They know they choose their behavior. Reactive people, on the other hand, are often affected by their physical environment. They find external sources to blame for their behavior. If the weather is good, they feel good. If it isn't, it affects their attitude and performance, and they blame the weather. All of these external forces act as stimuli that we respond to. Between the stimulus and the response is your greatest power—you have the freedom to choose your response. One of the most important things you choose is what you say. Your language is a good indicator of how you see yourself. A proactive person uses proactive language—I can, I will, I prefer, etc. A reactive person uses reactive language—I can't, I have to, if only. Reactive people believe they are not responsible for what they say and do—they have no choice.

Instead of reacting to or worrying about conditions over which they have little or no control, proactive people focus their time and energy on things they can control. The problems, challenges, and opportunities we face fall into two areas—Circle of Concern and Circle of Influence.

Proactive people focus their efforts on their Circle of Influence. They work on the things they can do something about: health, children, problems at work. Reactive people focus their efforts in the Circle of Concern—things over which they have little or no control: the national debt, terrorism, the weather. Gaining an awareness of the areas in which we expend our energies in is a giant step in becoming proactive.

Habit 2: Begin with the End in Mind

Develop a principle-centered personal mission statement. Extend the mission statement into long-term goals based on personal principles. Begin with the End in Mind So, what do you want to be when you grow up? That question may appear a little trite, but think about it for a moment. Are you—right now—who you want to be, what you dreamed you'd be, doing what you always wanted to do? Be honest. Sometimes people find themselves achieving victories that are empty—successes that have come at the expense of things that were far more valuable to them. If your ladder is not leaning against the right wall, every step you take gets you to the wrong place faster.

Habit 2 is based on imagination—the ability to envision in your mind what you cannot at present see with your eyes. It is based on the principle that all things are created twice. There is a mental (first) creation, and a physical (second) creation. The physical creation follows the mental, just as a building follows a blueprint. If you don't make a conscious effort to visualize who you are and what you want in life, then you empower other people and circumstances to shape you and your life by default. It's about connecting again with your own uniqueness and then defining the personal, moral, and ethical guidelines within which you can most happily express and fulfill. Begin with the End in Mind means to begin each day, task, or project with a clear vision of your desired direction and destination, and then continue by flexing your proactive muscles to make things happen. One of the best ways to incorporate Habit 2 into your life is to develop a Personal Mission Statement. It focuses on what you want to be and do. It is your plan for success. It reaffirms who you are, puts your goals in focus, and moves your ideas into the real world. Your mission statement makes you the leader of your own life. You create your own destiny and secure the future you envision.

Habit 3: Put First Things First

Spend time doing what fits into your personal mission, observing the proper balance between productions and building production capacity. Identify the key roles that you take on in life, and make time for each of them. Put First Things First to live a more balanced existence; you have to recognize that not doing everything that comes along is okay. There's no need to overextend you. All it takes is realizing that it's all right to say no when necessary and then focus on your highest priorities.

Habit 1 says, "You're in charge. You're the creator." Being proactive is about choice. Habit 2 is the first, or mental, creation. Beginning with the End in Mind is about vision. Habit 3 is the second creation, the physical creation. This habit is where Habits 1 and 2 come together. It happens day in and day out, moment-by-moment. It deals with many of the questions addressed in the field of time management. But that's not all it's about. Habit 3 is about life management as well—your purpose, values, roles, and priorities. What are "first things?" First things are those things you, personally, find of most worth. If you put first things first, you are organizing and managing time and events according to the personal priorities you established in Habit 2.

Habit 4: Think Win/Win

Seek agreements and relationships that are mutually beneficial. In cases where a "win/win" deal cannot be achieved, accept the fact that agreeing to make "no deal" may be the best alternative. In developing an organizational culture, be sure to reward win.

Think Win-Win isn't about being nice, nor is it a quick-fix technique. It is a character-based code for human interaction and collaboration. Most of us learn to base our self-worth on comparisons and competition. We think about succeeding in terms of someone else failing—that is, if I win, you lose; or if you win, I lose. Life becomes a zero-sum game. There is only so much pie to go around, and if you get a big piece, there is less for me; it's not fair, and I'm going to make sure you don't get anymore. We all play the game, but how much fun is it really? Win-win sees life as a cooperative arena, not a competitive one. Win-win is a frame of mind and heart that constantly seeks mutual benefit in all human interactions. Win-win means agreements or solutions are mutually beneficial and satisfying. We both get to eat the pie and it tastes pretty darn good! A person or organization that approaches conflicts with a win-win attitude possesses three vital character traits:

1. *Integrity:* sticking with your true feelings, values, and commitments.
2. *Maturity:* expressing your ideas and feelings with courage and consideration for the ideas and feelings of others.
3. *Abundance Mentality:* believing there is plenty for everyone.

Many people think in terms of either/or: either you're nice or you're tough. Win-win requires that you be both. It is a balancing act between courage and consideration. To go for win-win, you not only have to be empathic, but you also have to be confident. You not only have to be considerate and sensitive, you also have to be brave. To do that—to achieve that balance between courage and consideration—is the essence of real maturity and is fundamental to win-win.

Habit 5: Seek First to Understand, Then to Be Understood

First seek to understand the other person, and only then try to be understood. Stephen Covey presents this habit as the most important principle of interpersonal relations. Effective listening is not simply echoing what the other person has said through the lens of one's own experience. Rather, it is putting oneself in the perspective of the other person, listening empathically for both feeling and meaning. Communication is the most important skill in life. You spend years learning how to read and write, and years learning how to speak. But what about listening? What training have you had that enables you to listen so you really, deeply understand another human being? Probably none, right?

If you're like most people, you probably seek first to be understood; you want to get your point across. And in doing so, you may ignore the other person completely, pretend that you're listening, selectively hear only certain parts of the conversation or attentively focus on only the words being said, but miss the meaning entirely. So why does this happen? Because most people listen with the intent to reply, not to understand. You listen to yourself as you prepare in your mind what you are going to say, the questions you are going to ask, etc. You filter everything you hear through your life experiences, your frame of reference. You check what you hear against your autobiography and see how it measures up. And consequently, you decide prematurely what the other person means before he/she finishes communicating. Do any of the following sound familiar? "Oh, I know just how you feel. I felt the same way." "I had that same thing happen to me." "Let me tell you what I did in a similar situation." Because you so often listen autobiographically, you tend to respond in one of four ways:

Evaluating: You judge and then either agree or disagree.

Probing: You ask questions from your own frame of reference.

Advising: You give counsel, advice, and solutions to problems.

Interpreting: You analyze others' motives and behaviors based on your own experiences.

You might be saying, "Hey, now wait a minute. I'm just trying to relate to the person by drawing on my own experiences. Is that so bad?" In some situations, autobiographical responses may be appropriate, such as when another person specifically asks for help from your point of view or when there is already a very high level of trust in the relationship.

Habit 6: Synergize

Through trustful communication, find ways to leverage individual differences to create a whole that is greater than the sum of the parts. Through mutual trust and understanding, one often can solve conflicts and find a better solution than would have been obtained through either person's own solution.

To put it simply, synergy means "two heads are better than one." Synergize is the habit of creative cooperation. It is teamwork, open-mindedness, and the adventure of finding new solutions to old problems. But it doesn't just happen on its own. It's a process, and through that process, people bring all their personal experience and expertise to the table. Together, they can produce far better results that they could individually. Synergy lets us discover jointly things we are much less likely to discover by ourselves. It is the idea that the whole is greater than the sum of the parts. One plus one equals three, or six, or sixty—you name it.

When people begin to interact together genuinely, and they're open to each other's influence, they begin to gain new insight. The capability of inventing new approaches is increased exponentially because of differences. Valuing differences is what really drives synergy. Do you truly value the mental, emotional, and psychological differences among people? Or do you wish everyone would just agree with you so you could all get along? Many people mistake uniformity for unity; sameness for oneness. One word—boring! Differences should be seen as strengths, not weaknesses. They add zest to life.

Habit 7: Sharpen the Saw

Take time out from production to build production capacity through personal renewal of the physical, mental, social/emotional, and spiritual dimensions. Maintain a balance among these dimensions. Sharpen the Saw means preserving and enhancing the greatest asset you have—you. It means having a balanced program for self-renewal in the four areas of your life: physical, social/emotional, mental, and spiritual. Here are some examples of activities:

Physical: Beneficial eating, exercising, and resting

Social/Emotional: Making social and meaningful connections with others

Mental: Learning, reading, writing, and teaching

Spiritual: Spending time in nature, expanding spiritual self through meditation, music, art, prayer, or service

As you renew yourself in each of the four areas, you create growth and change in your life. Sharpen the Saw keeps you fresh so you can continue to practice the other six habits. You increase your capacity to produce and handle the challenges around you. Without this renewal, the body becomes weak, the mind mechanical, the emotions raw, the spirit insensitive, and the person selfish. Not a pretty picture, is it? Feeling good doesn't just happen. Living a life in balance means taking the necessary time to renew you. It's all up to you. You can renew yourself through relaxation. Or you can totally burn yourself out by overdoing everything. You can pamper yourself mentally and spiritually. Or you can go through life oblivious to your well-being. You can experience vibrant energy. Or you can procrastinate and miss out on the benefits of good health and exercise. You can revitalize yourself and face a new day in peace and harmony. Or you can wake up in the morning full of apathy because your get-up-and-go has got-up-and-gone. Just remember that every day provides a new opportunity for renewal – a new opportunity to recharge you instead of hitting the wall. All it takes is the desire, knowledge, and skill.

The 8th Habit: From Effectiveness to Greatness In today's challenging and complex world, being highly effective is the price of entry to the playing field. To thrive, innovate, excel, and lead in this new reality, we must reach beyond effectiveness toward fulfillment, contribution, and greatness. Research is showing, however, that the majority of people are not thriving. They are neither fulfilled nor excited. Tapping into the higher reaches of human motivation requires a new mindset, a new skill-set – a new habit. Dr.Covey's new book, *The 8th Habi: From Effectiveness to Greatness*, is a roadmap to help you find daily fulfillment and excitement.

Hierarchy of Human Needs

Abraham Maslow (April 1, 1908 - June 8, 1970) was an American psychologist. He is noted for his conceptualization of a "hierarchy of human needs", and is considered the founder of humanistic psychology.

Biography

Born and raised in Brooklyn, New York, Maslow was the oldest of seven children. His parents were uneducated Jews from Russia. He was slow and tidy, and remembered his childhood as lonely and rather unhappy, because, as he said, "I was the little Jewish boy in the non-Jewish neighborhood. It was a little like being the first Negro enrolled in the all-white school. I was isolated and unhappy. I grew up in libraries and among books, without friends." He would pursue law, but he went to graduate school at the University of Wisconsin to study psychology. While there, he married his first cousin Bertha in December 1928, and found as his chief mentor, Professor Harry Harlow. At Wisconsin he pursued an original line of research, investigating primate dominance behaviour and sexuality. He went on to further research at Columbia University, continuing similar studies; there he found another mentor in Alfred Adler, one of Sigmund Freud's early colleagues.

From 1937 to 1951, Maslow was on the faculty of Brooklyn College. In New York he found two more mentors, anthropologist Ruth Benedict and Gestalt psychologist Max Wertheimer, whom he admired both professionally and personally. These two were so accomplished in both realms and such "wonderful human beings" as well, that Maslow began taking notes about them and their behaviour. This would be the basis of his lifelong research and thinking about mental health and human potential. He wrote extensively on the subject, borrowing ideas from other psychologists but adding significantly to them, especially the concepts of a hierarchy of needs, metaneeds, self-actualizing persons, and peak experiences. Maslow became the leader of the humanistic school of psychology that emerged in the 1950s and 1960s, which he referred to as the "third force"—beyond Freudian theory and behaviourism.

Maslow was a professor at Brandeis University from 1951 to 1969, and then became a resident fellow of the Laughlin Institute in California. He died of a heart attack on June 8, 1970. In 1967, the American Humanist Association named him Humanist of the Year.

Humanistic Theories of Self Actualization

Many psychologists have made significant impacts on society's understanding of the world. Abraham Maslow was one of these; he brought a new face to the study of human behavior. He was inspired by great minds, and his own gift of thought created a unique concept of Humanistic Psychology. His family life and his experiences influenced the ideas that created a whole new form of psychology. After World War II, Maslow began to question the way psychologists had come to their conclusions, and though he didn't completely disagree, he had his own ideas on how to understand the Human mind. (The Developing Person through the Life Span, (1983), p. 42)

Humanistic Psychologists believe that every person has a strong desire to realize his or her full potential, to reach a level of Self-actualization. To prove that humans are not simply blindly reacting to situations, but trying to accomplish something greater, Maslow studied mentally healthy individuals instead of people with serious psychological issues. This enabled him to discover that people experience "peak experiences", high points in life when the individual is in harmony with himself and his surroundings. Self-actualized people can have many peak experiences throughout a day while others have those experiences less frequently. (The Developing Person through the Life Span, (1983) pg. 43)

A visual aid Maslow created to explain his theory, which he called the Hierarchy of Needs, is a pyramid depicting the levels of human needs, psychological and physical. When a human being ascends the steps of the pyramid he reaches self actualization. At the bottom of the pyramid are the "Basic needs" of a human being, food and water and touch. The next level is "Security and Stability." These two steps are important to the physical survival of the person. Once individuals have basic nutrition, shelter and safety, they attempt to accomplish more. The third level of need is "Love and Belonging," which are psychological needs; when individuals have taken care of themselves physically, they are ready to share themselves with others. The fourth level is achieved when individuals feel comfortable with what they have accomplished. This is the "Esteem" level, the level of success and status. The top of the pyramid, "Self-actualization," occurs when individuals reach a state of harmony and understanding. (The Developing Person through the Life Span, (1983) pg. 44)

Maslow based his study on magazines (e.g. "hello" and "Look") and the writings of other psychologists, including Albert Einstein, as well as people he knew who clearly met the standard of self actualization. Maslow used Einstein's writings and accomplishments to exemplify the characteristics of the self actualized person. He realized that all the individuals he studied had similar personality traits. All were "reality centered," able to differentiate what was fraudulent from what was genuine. They were also "problem centered," meaning that they treated life's difficulties as problems that demanded solutions. These individuals also were comfortable being alone and had healthy personal relationships. They had only a few close friends and family rather than a large number of shallow relationships. One historical figure Maslow found to be helpful in his journey to understanding self actualization was Lao Tzu, The Father of Taoism. A tenet of Taoism is that people do not obtain personal meaning or pleasure by seeking material possessions.

When Maslow introduced these ideas some weren't ready to understand them; others dismissed them as unscientific, a critique often leveled at Freud. Sometimes viewed as disagreeing with Freud and psychoanalytic theory, Maslow actually positioned his work as a vital complement to that of Freud. Maslow stated in his book, "It is as if Freud supplied us the sick half of psychology and we must now fill it out with the healthy half." (Toward a psychology of being, 1968) There are two faces of human nature-the sick and the healthy-so there should be two faces of psychology. Consequently, Maslow argued, the way in which essential needs are fulfilled is just as important as the needs themselves. Together, these define the human experience. To the extent a person finds cooperative social fulfillment, he establishes meaningful relationships with other people and the larger world. In other words, he establishes meaningful connections to an external reality-an essential component of self-actualization. In contrast, to the extent that vital needs find selfish and competitive fulfillment, a person acquires hostile emotions and limited external relationships-his awareness remains internal and limited.

Benedict and Wertheimer were Maslow's models of self-actualization. From them he generalized that, among other characteristics, self-actualizing people tend to focus on problems outside themselves; have a clear sense of what is true and what is false; are spontaneous and creative; and are not bound too strictly by social conventions. Beyond the routine of needs fulfillment, Maslow envisioned moments of extraordinary experience, known as Peak experiences, which are profound moments of love, understanding, happiness, or rapture, during which a person feels more whole, alive, self-sufficient and yet a part of the world, more aware of truth, justice, harmony, goodness, and so on. Self-actualizing people have many such peak experiences.

Maslow's thinking was surprisingly original-most psychologists before him had been concerned with the abnormal and the ill. He wanted to know what constituted positive mental health. Humanistic psychology gave rise to several different therapies, all guided by the idea that people possess the inner resources for growth and healing and that the point of therapy is to help remove obstacles to individuals' achieving them. The most famous of these was client-centered therapy developed by Carl Rogers. Classical Adlerian Psychotherapy, based on the teachings of Alfred Adler, also encourages the optimal psychological development of the individual. Maslow's influence extended beyond psychology - his work on peak experiences is relevant to religious studies, while his work on management is applicable to transpersonal business studies.

Hierarchy of Needs

Maslow has set up a hierarchy of five levels of basic needs. Beyond these needs, higher levels of needs exist. These include needs for understanding, aesthetic appreciation and purely spiritual needs. In the levels of the five basic needs, it is said that the person does not feel the second need until the demands of the first have been satisfied or the third until the second has been satisfied, and so on.

Writings

- *A Theory of Human Motivation* (originally published in *Psychological Review*, 1943, Vol. 50 #4, pp. 370–396).
- *Motivation and Personality* (1st edition: 1954, 2nd edition: 1970, 3rd edition 1987)
- *Religions, Values and Peak-experiences*, Columbus, Ohio: Ohio State University Press, 1964.
- *Eupsychian Management*, 1965; republished as *Maslow on Management*, 1998
- *The Psychology of Science: A Reconnaissance*, New York: Harper & Row, 1966; Chapel Hill: Maurice Bassett, 2002.
- *Toward a Psychology of Being*, (2nd edition, 1968)
- *The Farther Reaches of Human Nature*, 1971

Free Team Building Games Training Ideas and Tips

Free team building games ideas and theory for employee motivation, training and development. Here are techniques, theory and ideas for designing and using your own team building games, exercises and activities, and the free team building games, exercises and activities available in this site (free team building games are here - plus tips as to whether team building games and activities are suitable). Team building games, exercises and activities help build teams, develop employee motivation, improve communications and are fun - for corporate organizations, groups, children's development and even kids parties. Team building games, exercises, activities and quizzes also warm up meetings, improve training, and liven up conferences.

These free team building games ideas and rules will help you design and use games and exercises for training sessions, meetings, workshops, seminars or conferences, for adults, young people and children, in work, education or for clubs and social activities. Team building games, exercises and activities can also enhance business projects, giving specific business outputs and organizational benefits. We cannot accept responsibility for any liability which arises from the use of any of these free team building ideas or games - please see the disclaimer notice below. Always ensure that you have proper insurance in place for all team building games activities, and take extra care when working with younger people, children and organising kids party games.

Teamwork

Great teamwork makes things happen more than anything else in organizations. The diagram representing McGregor's X-Y Theory helps illustrate how and why empowered teams get the best results. Empowering people is more about attitude and behaviour towards staff than processes and tools. Teamwork is fostered by respecting, encouraging, enthusing, caring for people, not exploiting or dictating to them.

At the heart of this approach is love and spirituality which helps bring mutual respect, compassion, and humanity to work. People working for each other in teams are powerful force, more than skills, processes, policies. More than annual appraisals, management-by-objectives, the 'suits' from head office; more than anything. *Teams usually become great teams when they decide to do it for themselves* - not because someone says so. Something inspires them maybe, but ultimately the team decides. It's a team thing. It has to be. The team says: 'Okay. We can bloody well make a difference. We will be the best at what we do. We'll look out for each other and succeed - for us - for the team. And we'll make sure we enjoy ourselves while we're doing it'. And then the team starts to move mountains.

Using and Planning Team-building Activities

People are best motivated if you can involve them in designing and deciding the activities—ask them. Secondly you will gain most organisational benefit if the activities are geared towards developing people's own potential—find out what they will enjoy doing and learning. Games can be trite or patronising for many people—they want activities that will help them learn and develop in areas that interest them for life, beyond work stuff-again ask them. When you ask people commonly you'll have several suggestions which can be put together as a collection of experiences that people attend or participate in on a rotating basis during the day or the team-building event. Perhaps you have people among your employees who themselves have special expertise or interests which they'd enjoy sharing with others; great team activities can be built around many hobbies and special interests. If you are planning a whole day of team-building activities bear in mind that a whole day of 'games' is a waste of having everyone together for a whole day. Find ways to provide a mix of activities that appeal and help people achieve and learn—maybe build in exercises focusing on one or two real work challenges or opportunities, using a workshop approach. Perhaps involve a few employees in planning the day (under your guidance or not according to the appropriate level of delegated authority)—it will be good for their own development and will lighten your load. See also the guide to facilitating experiential learning activities.

Team Exercises and Events for Developing Ethical Organizations

Team-building exercises and activities also provide a wonderful opportunity to *bring to life the increasing awareness and interest in 'ethical organizations'*. These modern ethical business ideas and concepts of sustainability, 'Fairtrade', corporate social responsibility, the 'triple bottom line', love, compassion, humanity and spirituality, etc., are still not well defined or understood: people are unclear what it all means for them individually and for the organization as a whole, even though most people are instinctively attracted to the principles. Team-exercises and discussions help bring clarity and context to idealistic concepts like ethics and social responsibility far more effectively than reading the theory, or trying to assimilate some airy-fairy new mission statement dreamed up by someone at head office and handed down as an edict. Fundamental change has to come from within, with support from above sure, but *successful change is ultimately successful because people 'own' it and see it as their change,* not something handed down. See for example the Triple Bottom Line exercise.

Ensure that team-building activities and all corporate events comply with equality and discrimination policy and law in respect of gender, race, disability, age, etc. Age discrimination is a potential risk given certain groups and activities, and particularly so because Age Discrimination is quite a recent area of legislation. Team-building facilitators should be familiar with the Employment Equality Age Regulations, effective 1st October 2006. While this is UK and European legislation, the principles are applicable to planning and running team-building exercises anywhere in the world, being consistent with the ethical concepts.

Corporate Events and Social Responsibility

Also consider the effects of team building and corporate events in terms of effects on employees' families and people's broader life needs. It is easy to become very narrowly focused on the organization and the community within it, without thinking of the families and social needs outside. Alcohol is another increasing area of risk for organizers of team building and conference events. An employer's duty of care (and potential liability) at corporate events traditionally was fulfilled by ensuring no-one tripped over the electrical cable for the overhead projector. Nowadays organizations have a deeper wider responsibility, which is progressively reflected in law. Alcohol and discrimination are big issues obviously, but arguably a bigger responsibility for employers is to the families and social well-being of employees, which impacts directly onto society as a whole.

Today's well-led and ethically-managed corporations understand that divisive treatment of employees' partners and families undermines loyalty and motivation of employees, and creates additional unnecessary stresses for workers in close loving caring relationships, especially for young families, which have evolved a strong sensitivity to such pressures. If you read about Erik Erikson's Life Stages Theory you will understand why parents of young children especially are not helped by this sort of work pressure. Thwarting or obstructing people's instincts—evolved over millennia—to be with and take care of their partners and young families is extremely destructive. Employers who have a blatant antipathy for these crucial life needs of their people are therefore socially irresponsible.

Inevitably strong work commitments put pressure on employees' families and partners. This is particularly so in big modern corporations where travel and lengthy absence from home is unavoidable in key roles. Modern ethical socially responsible organizations should be doing whatever they can to minimize these effects, not make them worse. Where possible employers should reward partners and families for their support and loyalty, rather than alienate them by creating selfish staff-only events. Laws are not yet clearly defined about the employer's liabilities arising from such situations, however there are clear principles (e.g., related to stress, duty of care, social responsibility, etc.) which demand responsibility and anticipation from employers in this area. Moreover, fostering a healthy work and home life balance tends to make organizations run smoother and less problematically, notably in areas of grievance and counseling, stress and conflict, disputes and litigation, recruitment and staff retention, succession planning, company reputation and image.

Risks and Dangers of Socially Irresponsible Events and Activities

I was prompted to add this item because I received a question about the implications of running a staff-only dinner dance at a conference event. If you are considering a staff-only social event—especially at night, involving alcohol and dancing, overnight accommodation—or you are wondering generally where to draw the line between working relationships and intimacy, or between fun and irresponsible risk, these observations might help you decide. Implications and risks of organizing socially irresponsible events concern chiefly:

1. Romantic/sexual relations between staff, whether extra-marital or not.
2. Stresses on partners and families and thereby on staff too, if partners are excluded from intimate social events.
3. Problems, accidents, incidents arising from alcohol.
4. Impacts on performance, management distraction, and staff retention arising from the above.
5. Risks of litigation and bad publicity arising from any of the above.

The risks of running a socially irresponsible corporate event are emphasised if you consider a scenario containing the following elements. Do not run an event containing these elements. This is a negative example for the purposes of illustrating risk and responsibility:

1. Evening dinner and dance or disco.
2. Dressing up—especially black tie, long dresses (and whatever the women will be wearing—no, seriously..)
3. A bar, or other access to alcohol (the more freely available then the more risk).
4. Overnight accommodation.
5. Heady atmosphere of achievement, motivation, team-working, relationship-building and general showing off (many conference events contain these features, especially those aiming to motivate, reward, entertain, etc., and especially events for staff involved in sales, management and the more extroverted people-oriented roles within organizations).
6. Scheduled on the last night of the event (sense of climax, relief, tension release, "...Tomorrow it all ends and back to normal..." etc.)
7. Partners excluded (for whatever reason - either because the CEO is a thrice married and divorced dirty old man, or because the event necessarily brings delegates together from a wide geographical area, which prevents partners attending due to logistics and costs).

You do not need to be a professor of social anthropology to guess that the above circumstances are unlikely to be a useful corporate defence against any of the following problems which could arise, directly, indirectly, or ironically if actually nothing whatever to do with the event itself—try telling that to the offended party afterwards...

1. Extra-marital liaisons of various sorts between various people away from home, whether serial philanderers, or momentarily weak in the face of temptation.

2. Seductions or more serious sexual behaviours resulting in a victim or complaint of some sort.
3. Abuse of power/authority/bar-tab by a senior staff member, resulting in scandal when a junior victim subsequently emerges, and says it all happened because they got drunk downing umpteen free sambucas with the directors and then got taken advantage of.
4. Someone decides to drive away on the night three or four times over the legal limit and getting arrested or causing an accident.
5. Damage to person or property, or violence resulting from too much alcohol.

You could probably add to this list. There is no limit to human ingenuity when behaving irresponsibly under the influence of drink and any other stimulants of emotion or substance. A socially responsible employer should be able to demonstrate they have been duly careful and diligent in minimizing such risks when organizing any work events.

Excluding Partners from Events...

Executives, managers and employees of successful organizations hopefully love their work. They live and breathe it, which is great—but what about the partners and families? Do they love the organization? Usually not. Overly demanding work is a threat to family life—and thereby to society. And just because a few staff members and crusty old directors can't wait to get away from their spouses (a feeling no doubt reciprocated by the spouses), doesn't mean that all employees feel the same way. The vast majority do not. Staging intense social staff-only events can be deeply upsetting to employees' partners and families, whose interests are nowadays (and arguably as ever) firmly within an employer's duty of care and social responsibility. Divorce, separation and family conflicts and breakdowns are directly linked with many social ills. Socially responsible ethical employers should be doing all they can to reduce these causal factors—not to make them worse. Remind yourself of Maslow's Hierarchy of Needs if you are in doubt about the acute stress which arises when anyone is threatened at the level of family, loving relationships, home, etc. Consider the stresses and difficulties caused to employees' partners excluded from such occasions, and the effects which inevitably rebound on the employees, and cascade to children. These are truly basic needs and an organization which jeopardises these factors is irresponsible in the extreme. Here are some examples of different resources which can be used in creating teambuilding events and activities.

Free team building games, exercises, activities and ideas—for adults and children's party games too more teambuilding activities ideas free quizzes—questions and answers—trivia, general knowledge, and management and business quiz free motivational and amusing posters—ideas for themes and maxims to underpin team-building how to run workshops—tips for motivational, development and team-building workshops buddha maitreya's japanese garden and meditation centre—an example of an innovative venue for team activities and events fantasticat—the Fantasticat ideas for motivating, teaching and developing young people—grown-ups too.. role playing process and tips—for role play games and exercises see also the free puzzles and tricks—ideal for team building exercises and the training and business acronyms for more team building and training sessions ideas. If you are a manager, supervisor or team leader, and are wondering *how to select a team building activity,* an easy and effective way to begin the process is to simply *ask the team* what sort of activity they would prefer. For example—do they want to play games, or would the team prefer to use an activity that focuses on a work issue, or work skills, in the way that workshops can do. Asking a team what they want to is particularly relevant if the team is mature and/or contains mature team members.

Younger inexperienced teams will need more guidance and perhaps a list of possibilities to choose from.

Involving the team in deciding what activities to use is empowering and participative, and will help to lighten your management load. Refer to, explain and remember the POB acronym, which is a great mnemonic (memory aid) to reinforce the need for all team members to be involved and engaged in team work-teams work best when everyone contributes—which means no passengers. It's the team leaders, or managers, or facilitator's responsibility to structure and help teams to ensure that all team members have the opportunity and incentive to contribute and participate in team activities, and ultimately the team's success. It is helpful to use and refer to these models when using, planning, designing, and evaluating team building activities or games:

- Kirkpatrick's learning evaluation model,
- Bloom's Taxonomy of learning domains

Introducing team members to Kirkpatrick's and Bloom's concepts can also help them to develop a clearer understanding of their own needs, and their preferred methods of training and development—individually and for the team. And here are some tips for more conventional team building activities:

- Practice the team building exercise yourself first to check that it works, check timings, materials, and to ensure you have all the answers. Anticipation and planning are vital.
- Make sure all team building games instructions are clear and complete - essential for keeping control and credibility.
- Become proficient yourself first with any team building games or equipment that you use.
- Always have spare materials and equipment to allow for more people, breakages and the inevitable

requests for freebie items ("Can I take a couple home for my kids?...")

- Take extra care when organising teambuilding activities and games for young people, especially kids activities and children's party games.
- Attaching a theme to team-building activities helps make the exercises more memorable—see the free motivational posters for ideas and examples tips for quick games and exercises for warm-ups and team building

First of all—use your imagination—you can simplify, adapt, shorten and lengthen most games and exercises. To turn a long complex game into a quick activity or warm-up, scale down the materials, shorten the time allowed, and make the exercise easier. Most of the games on the free games page can also be used for children's education and development, and for kids party games—adapt them to suit. The number of members per team affects activity time and complexity—teams of four or more need a leader and tends to take longer than a pair or team of three. Increasing or reducing team size, and introducing or removing the team-leader requirement, are simple ideas for increasing or reducing game complexity and exercise duration.

Whatever you choose, as the facilitator, practice it yourself first so you anticipate all the possible confusions, and so that you have a good idea of how best to do it (you'll generally be asked by the delegates after the exercise). Think carefully about team sizes - pairs or teams of three are best for short 'construction' exercises, unless you want a leadership element in the game. Without a leader, too many team members cause non-participation and chaos, so avoid this (unless the purpose of the exercise is to demonstrate why teams need leadership). For a quick game any newspaper construction exercises in pairs is good—if people have done the exercise before add an extra challenge aspect to make it different (maybe give each team a banana to support on top of the construction and/or limit the team to just 2 or three sheets of paper, or ban the use of sticky tape) - whatever, if you have a slot of 20 mines, allow 10 minutes for the exercise so as not to rush the introductory explanation or the review. Remember your tape measure, and practice the activity yourself to try to come up with an ideal solution for when they ask at the review. Alternatively pick three or four lateral thinking puzzles and split the group into two teams. Use quizzes too. Larger teams are fine for quizzes because team working is less crucial. Giving a tight deadline will encourage the teams to share out the puzzles, which emphasises leadership, communication and use of skills and resources. Think about the points that the exercise are illustrating so you can review afterwards sensibly.

Tips for Working with Syndicate Groups for Team Building or Training

Team building games and training exercises work better using syndicate groups, or teams. This is particularly so if you want a competitive element, which is very effective in building teams and team spirit. Working with syndicates also encourages and enables more participation, activity and ideas, and managed well, it makes the trainer's or facilitator's job easier. Using syndicates in team building needs thought and planning - here are some pointers:

- think about what you are trying to achieve and structure the teams accordingly.
- always plan in advance how you intend to structure the syndicates.
- threes work best when you want everyone to be involved. pairs ensure everyone is involved, and generally work quicker than threes, but are less dynamic than threes.
- groups above threes will require a leader to emerge or people will be left out.

- groups of four or five are good for providing the opportunity for leaders to emerge.
- groups of six or more require quite competent leadership skills within the group.
- ensure clear instructions are given to each syndicate, and these are best given in writing as well.
- more pressure is put on the team if only one set of instructions is given - less pressure results from giving each team member a copy of the task instructions.
- the best number of team members to achieve a certain effect will vary according to each exercise or game or activity.
- you can change or keep the make-up of the syndicates as you change exercises, depending on the precise team building and relationship aims.
- some people are not comfortable being in the same team or group as their subordinates or manager.
- you have the option to nominate individuals to perform certain functions within the team, egg time-keeping, leading, scribe (recording), communicating, etc.
- ensure syndicates have necessary equipment and materials, depending on format - e.g. flip chart paper, pens, laptop, acetates.
- ensure suitable space and working area exists for the number and size of syndicates you plan to work with.

These ideas concern training people (or learning for yourself) to become a great team building facilitator. The job of training managers and trainers how to run team building sessions is different to running a team-building session per se. It's important that delegates experience the effect of different types of team building, and also and the effect of the many variables which might apply (team numbers, mix, location etc); different types of games and exercises and their purpose (games, quizzes, competitions, warm-ups, exercises, workshops, etc), and the theory surrounding team building and designing team building activities (personality and psychometrics; leadership; communications; planning and preparation; follow-up; stress, fun and physical activity; etc). Becoming an expert in team building is a wonderful career specialty to pursue. The growing popularity of team building, and the recognition of structured, organized team building as a significant factor in the performance and well-being of individuals, teams and organizations, will fuel growth in demand for, and provision of, specialist team building training. (If you can recommend any particularly good team building design/facilitation training courses do let me know.)

Team building potentially includes a very wide variety of methodologies, techniques, theories and tools. And also values and philosophy. At the foundation of good team building is compassion and humanity - genuine care for others. This is what sustains and fuels people in organizations. It follows then that to become a great team builder you should open yourself to philosophical ideas and values, as well as learn and experience as many methodologies and related techniques as you can, which together will combine to give you the character, skills and breadth for becoming an inspirational leader in team building - and in the training of team building to others, be they trainers, managers, facilitators or team leaders. Here are some examples of useful methodologies, concepts, etc. that is useful for anyone involved in team building:

- Facilitation is a key element - and there are some quite advanced techniques surfacing in this area now - beyond organising groups, rooms and refreshments etc., for example Jim Rough's excellent 'Dynamic Facilitation' concept.
- Look at Kirkpatrick's learning evaluation model

- Also look at Bloom's Taxonomy of learning domains
- Train the trainer courses—many and various, from the inspirational to more theoretical—include lots of relevant learning about working with groups.
- Consider and talk about the growing importance of love and spirituality in organizations.
- Motivational and communications methodologies such as NLP, and Transactional Analysis.
- Psychometrics (personality testing) and team role understanding.
- Sports psychology contains some really useful and relevant elements.
- So do meditation and belief.
- So do modern life-balance philosophies such as the thinking of Cherie Carter-Scott, and Don Miguel Ruiz.
- Outdoor survival, 'outward bound' courses, and personal challenge activities are also useful to experience and understand, in terms of what they offer people and how the process develops at a deep level.
- And always remember the importance of fun, games and toys—for example juggling, plate-spinning, board games, tricks, puzzles, etc., use your imagination—school education suppliers and exhibitions can be a really useful source of ideas, providers and new products.

Whether you find a dedicated team building trainer/ facilitation course or not I'd recommend you access as many of the above sorts of methodologies and concepts—and anything else that inspires and stimulates—whenever the opportunity arises. When planning and running team building activities, exercises, games, etc., certain variables have a significant influence on the way the activity works. When planning team building—or any group activity—think about and use these factors to suit the situation, logistics, team/ group numbers, and the aims of the exercises.

- team mix (age, job type, department, gender, seniority, etc)
- team numbers (one to a hundred or more, pairs and threes, leadership issues)
- exercise briefing and instructions - how difficult you make the task, how full the instructions and clues are
- games or exercise duration
- competitions and prizes
- venue and logistics - room size and availability (for break-out sessions etc)
- materials provided or available
- stipulation of team member roles - e.g., team leader, time-keeper, scribe (note-taker), reviewer/presenter
- scoring, and whether the exercise is part of an ongoing competition or team league

With a full day or more it's very useful to include something on personality types and how this affects teams, style of management required, learning styles (e.g. Kolb, VAK, etc). If you use psychometrics in your organization, if possible expose delegates to the testing and theory—it's interesting and a great basis for absorbing the issues. It also adds a bit of hard theory to the inevitable other soft content. Ongoing competitions are excellent for team building, but If you are training the trainers don't run a competition through the whole day—mix up the teams from time to time to show how team dynamics can be changed and the effect of doing so. Also demonstrate how games take on a different meaning if numbers are changed (e.g. larger teams require leadership or there'll be passengers (see the POB team-building acronym); and, you can play the same game with 3 and 6 people and it completely alters the conduct and outcomes). Change and demonstrate gender and age mixes also - team mix is a crucial area of understanding.

Use a mixture of games to cover different logistical and environmental constraints - small room, large room, syndicate rooms, outdoors. Include a mixture of games to develop different skills and aspects within team building - leadership, cooperation, communication, breaking down barriers, planning, time-management, etc. Ask the delegates (in syndicates) to design their own games to meet specific scenarios. As well as the ideas, look at all the variables: clarity of instructions, timings, team numbers and mix, logistics, venue requirements, etc. Outdoors, use traditional games like rounder, cricket, touch rugby, relay races, to demonstrate the big team dynamics, and the physical exercise effect - stress reduction, endorphins and neuro-transmitters, etc. Also cover 'workshops' and how to plan and run them - practical sessions dealing with real business issues, with real content and real action-based outcomes, including the team-building effect - use a real business issue as an example. This would also require some pre-session preparation and coached and measurable follow-up, which are also extremely useful and under-used mechanisms.

Here's a simple easy tip for team-building, motivation, and creating happy atmosphere: Buy a big basket. Buy lots of sweets or candy, lollipops too, wrapped preferably (for hygiene and maintenance reasons) and put them into the big basket. Put the big basket of sweets and lollipops on the table before people arrive for work, or the meeting, or the training session. And then watch people smile. Sweets and lollipops break down barriers. They are a universal language for feeling good and being happy. After a week or two of different sweets throw in some bubblegum. Also some bubblegum with collectible cards. This gesture is not restricted to the training room; you can put baskets of sweets all over the place. Even in the reception and the board room; and even in the finance director's office. You can ask the receptionist if she (or he) would be so kind as to make sure that the sweet basket is always filled to the brim (at the company's cost of course), and to make sure she (or he) always invites every single visitor to dip their hand in and take a big handful for their kids. And you'll see how wonderfully well people react to being treated in this way. When you've firmly established the practice of having baskets of sweets everywhere, you can move on to fresh cut flowers.........A little bunch of fresh cut flowers in a vase, on a table. It's worth a million words. (Next of course you'll need to appoint a flower monitor, which every right-minded person will want to be, so you can have one per floor, or one per day of the week, or one per department, whatever...)

David c McClelland's Motivational Needs Theory

American David Clarence McClelland (1917-98) achieved his doctorate in psychology at Yale in 1941 and became professor at Wesleyan University. He then taught and lectured, including a spell at Harvard from 1956, where with colleagues for twenty years he studied particularly motivation and the achievement need. He began his McBer consultancy in 1963, helping industry assess and train staff, and later taught at Boston University, from 1987 until his death. McClelland is chiefly known for his work on achievement motivation, but his research interests extended to personality and consciousness. David McClelland pioneered workplace motivational thinking, developing achievement-based motivational theory and models, and promoted improvements in employee assessment methods, advocating competency-based assessments and tests, arguing them to be better than traditional IQ and personality-based tests. His ideas have since been widely adopted in many organisations, and relate closely to the theory of Frederick Herzberg. David McClelland is most noted for describing three types of motivational need, which he identified in his 1961 book, The Achieving Society:

- achievement motivation (n-ach)

- authority/power motivation (n-pow)
- affiliation motivation (n-affil)

David McClelland's Needs-based Motivational Model

These needs are found to varying degrees in all workers and managers, and this mix of motivational needs characterises a person's or manager's style and behaviour, both in terms of being motivated and in the management and motivation others.

The Need for Achievement (n-ach)

The n-ach person is 'achievement motivated' and therefore seeks achievement, attainment of realistic but challenging goals, and advancement in the job. There is a strong need for feedback as to achievement and progress, and a need for a sense of accomplishment.

The Need for Authority and Power (n-pow)

The n-pow person is 'authority motivated'. This driver produces a need to be influential, effective and to make an impact. There is a strong need to lead and for their ideas to prevail. There is also motivation and need towards increasing personal status and prestige.

The Need for Affiliation (n-affil)

The n-affil person is 'affiliation motivated', and has a need for friendly relationships and is motivated towards interaction with other people. The affiliation driver produces motivation and need to be liked and held in popular regard. These people are team players. McClelland said that most people possess and exhibit a combination of these characteristics. Some people exhibit a strong bias to a particular motivational need and this motivational or needs 'mix' consequently affects their behaviour and working/managing style. Mcclelland suggested that a strong n-affil 'affiliation-motivation' undermines a manager's objectivity, because of their need to be liked, and that this affects a manager's decision-making capability. A strong n-pow 'authority-motivation' will produce a determined work ethic and commitment to the organisation, and while n-pow people are attracted to the leadership role; they may not possess the required flexibility and people-centred skills. McClelland argues that n-ach people with strong 'achievement motivation' make the best leaders, although there can be a tendency to demand too much of their staff in the belief that they are all similarly and *highly* achievement-focused and results driven, which of course most people are not.

McClelland's particular fascination was for achievement motivation, and this laboratory experiment illustrates one aspect of his theory about the affect of achievement on people's motivation. McClelland asserted via this experiment that while most people do not possess a strong achievement-based motivation, those who do, display a consistent behaviour in setting goals: Volunteers were asked to throw rings over pegs rather like the fairground game; no distance was stipulated, and most people seemed to throw from arbitrary, random distances, sometimes close, sometimes farther away. However a small group of volunteers, whom McClelland suggested were strongly achievement-motivated, took some care to measure and test distances to produce an ideal challenge - not too easy, and not impossible. Interestingly a parallel exists in biology, known as the 'overload principle', which is commonly applied to fitness and exercising, i.e., in order to develop fitness and/or strength the exercise must be sufficiently demanding to increase existing levels, but not so demanding as to cause damage or strain. McClelland identified the same need for a 'balanced challenge' in the approach of achievement-motivated people.

McClelland contrasted achievement-motivated people with gamblers, and dispelled a common pre-conception that n-ach 'achievement-motivated' people are big risk takers. On the contrary - typically, achievement-motivated individuals set goals which they can influence with their effort and ability, and as such the goal is considered to be achievable. This determined results-driven approach is almost invariably present in the character make-up of all successful business people and entrepreneurs. McClelland suggested other characteristics and attitudes of achievement-motivated people:

- achievement is more important than material or financial reward.
- achieving the aim or task gives greater personal satisfaction than receiving praise or recognition.
- financial reward is regarded as a measurement of success, not an end in itself.
- security is not prime motivator, nor is status.
- feedback is essential, because it enables measurement of success, not for reasons of praise or recognition (the implication here is that feedback must be reliable, quantifiable and factual).
- achievement-motivated people constantly seek improvements and ways of doing things better.
- achievement-motivated people will logically favour jobs and responsibilities that naturally satisfy their needs, i.e. offer flexibility and opportunity to set and achieve goals, e.g., sales and business management, and entrepreneurial roles.

McClelland firmly believed that achievement-motivated people are generally the ones who make things happen and get results, and that this extends to getting results through the organisation of other people and resources, although as stated earlier, they often demand too much of their staff because they priorities achieving the goal above the many varied interests and needs of their people. Interesting comparisons and relationships can be drawn between McClelland's motivation types, and the characteristics defined in other behavioural models, e.g.: John Adair's Action-Centred Leadership model: Achievement-motivated managers are firmly focused on the Task, often to the detriment of the Individual and the Team. Affiliation-motivation people are Team and Individual centred. (Note that John Adair's Action-Centred leadership model is ©John Adair.) Katherine Benziger'sThinking Styles model: Achievement-motivation is a double-frontal brain mode style; affiliation-motivation is right basal (rear); authority-motivation is arguably left basal. DISC (Inscape, Thomas International, etc) system: Achieve-ment-motivated people are 'D' profiles - results-driven, decisive, dominant, etc. Affiliation-motivated people are I (proactive) and S (reactive) profiles. Authority-motivated people are S and C profiles.

Heresy/Blanchard's Situational Leadership® model: Achievement-motivated people tend to favour the styles of the first and second modes ('telling' and 'selling'); affiliation-motivated people tend to favour the third mode ('participating'); and the authority-motivated people tend to favour the style of mode four ('delegating'). Please note that Situational Leadership® is protected intellectual property: Situational Leadership® is a trademark of the Centre for Leadership Studies. Situational Leadership II® is a trademark of The Ken Blanchard Companies. Use of material relating to Situational Leadership® and/or Situational Leadership II® requires licence and agreement from the respective companies. McGregor XY Theory: Achievement-motivated people tend towards X-Theory style, due to their high task focus; there are plenty of exceptions however, and training definitely helps the n-ach manager to see the value of employing Theory Y style. n-pow managers are definitely Theory X. n-affil are typically Theory Y and if not can relatively easily be trained to be so. Herzberg motivators and hygiene factors: n-ach people are more responsive to the Herzberg motivators (especially achievement obviously) than n-affil and n-pow people.

John Adair's Action Centred Leadership - A Model for Team Leadership and Management

John Adair's simple Action-Centred Leadership model (action-centered if you prefer the US spelling) provides a great blueprint for leadership and the management of any team, group or organization. Action Centred Leadership is also a simple leadership and management model, which makes it easy to remember and apply, and to adapt for your own situation. Good managers and leaders should have full command of the three main areas of the Action Centred Leadership model, and should be able to use each of the elements according to the situation. Being able to do all of these things, and keep the right balance, gets results, builds morale, improves quality, develops teams and productivity, and is the mark of a successful manager and leader.

John Adair's Action-centred Leadership Model

The three parts of Adair's Action-Centred Leadership model are commonly represented by three overlapping circles, which is a trademark belonging to John Adair, and used here with his permission. Adair's famous 'three circles' model is one of the most recognizable and iconic symbols within management theory. When you refer to this diagram for teaching and training purposes please attribute it to John Adair, and help preserve the integrity and origins of this excellent model.

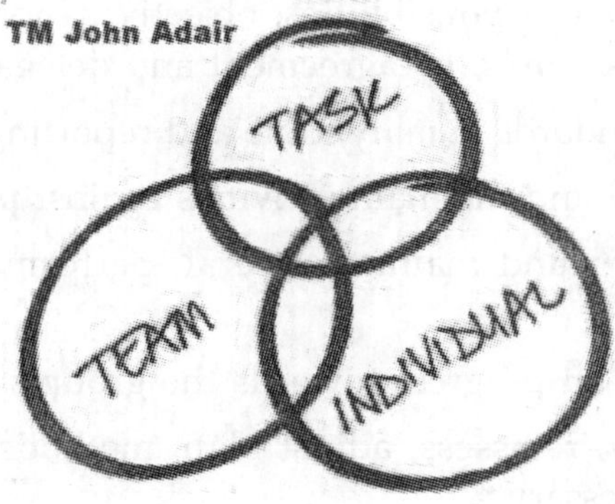

John Adair's Action-Centred Leadership model is represented by Adair's 'three circles' diagram, which illustrates Adair's three core management responsibilities:

- achieving the task
- managing the team or group
- managing individuals

John Adair's action-centred leadership task-team-individual model adapts extremely well (as below) for the demands of modern business management. When using it in your own environment think about the aspects of performance necessary for success in ***your own*** situation, and incorporate local relevant factors into the model to create your own interpretation. This will give you a very useful management framework:

Your responsibilities as a manager for achieving the task are:

- identify aims and vision for the group, purpose, and direction - define the activity (the task)
- identify resources, people, processes, systems and tools (inc. financials, communications, IT)
- create the plan to achieve the task - deliverables, measures, timescales, strategy and tactics
- establish responsibilities, objectives, accountabilities and measures, by agreement and delegation
- set standards, quality, time and reporting parameters
- control and maintain activities against parameters
- monitor and maintain overall performance against plan
- report on progress towards the group's aim
- review, re-assess, adjust plan, methods and targets as necessary

Your responsibilities as a manager for the group are:

- establish, agree and communicate standards of performance and behaviour
- establish style, culture, approach of the group - soft skill elements
- monitor and maintain discipline, ethics, integrity and focus on objectives
- anticipate and resolve group conflict, struggles or disagreements
- assess and change as necessary the balance and composition of the group
- develop team-working, cooperation, morale and team-spirit
- develop the collective maturity and capability of the group - progressively increase group freedom and authority
- encourage the team towards objectives and aims - motivate the group and provide a collective sense of purpose
- identify, develop and agree team- and project-leadership roles within group
- enable, facilitate and ensure effective internal and external group communications
- identify and meet group training needs
- give feedback to the group on overall progress; consult with, and seek feedback and input from the group

Your responsibilities as a manager for each individual are:

- understand the team members as individuals - personality, skills, strengths, needs, aims and fears
- assist and support individuals - plans, problems, challenges, highs and lows

- identify and agree appropriate individual responsibilities and objectives
- give recognition and praise to individuals - acknowledge effort and good work
- where appropriate reward individuals with extra responsibility, advancement and status
- identify, develop and utilise each individual's capabilities and strengths
- train and develop individual team members
- develop individual freedom and authority

Action Centered Leadership and John Adair

John Adair, born 1934, British, developed his Action Centred Leadership model while lecturing at Sandhurst Royal Military Academy and as assistant director and head of leadership department at The Industrial Society. This would have been during the 1960s and 70s, so in terms of management theories, Adair's works is relatively recent.

His work certainly encompasses and endorses much of the previous thinking on human needs and motivation by Maslow, Herzberg and Fayol, and his theory adds an elegant and simple additional organisational dimension to these earlier works. Very importantly, Adair was probably the first to demonstrate that leadership is a trainable, transferable skill, rather than it being an exclusively inborn ability. He helped change perception of management to encompass leadership, to include associated abilities of decision-making, communication and time-management. As well as developing the Action Centred Leadership model, Adair wrote over 40 books on management and leadership, including Effective Leadership, Not Bosses but Leaders, and Great Leaders.

Adair is now a management consultant and also has his own publishing company in Surrey, England. He also maintains links with the University of Surrey, where he was the first

UK chair of leadership studies, 1979-83. The John Adair Leadership Foundation appointed Dr David Farady as its director in January 2006. Carol Kennedy's excellent book 'Guide to the Management Gurus' supports the view that John Adair's ideas are fundamental and very significant in the development of management and leadership thinking: Leadership is different to management. All leaders are not necessarily great managers, but the best leaders will possess good management skills. One skill-set does not automatically imply the other will be present. Adair used the original word meanings to emphasise this: Leadership is an ancient ability about deciding direction, from an Anglo-Saxon word meaning the road or path ahead; knowing the next step and then taking others with you to it. Managing is a later concept, from Latin 'manus', meaning hand, and more associated with handling a system or machine of some kind. The original concept of managing began in the 19th century when engineers and accountants started to become entrepreneurs.

There are valuable elements of management not necessarily found in leadership, e.g. administration and managing resources. Leadership on the other hand contains elements not necessarily found in management, e.g., inspiring others through the leaders own enthusiasm and commitment. The Action Centred Leadership model is Adair's best known work, in which the three elements - Achieving the Task, Developing the Team and Developing Individuals - are mutually dependent, as well as being separately essential to the overall leadership role. Importantly as well, Adair set out these core functions of leadership and says they are vital to the Action Centered Leadership model:

- Planning - seeking information, defining tasks, setting aims Initiating - briefing, task allocation, setting standards
- Controlling - maintaining standards, ensuring progress, ongoing decision-making

- Supporting - individuals' contributions, encouraging, team spirit, reconciling, morale
- Informing - clarifying tasks and plans, updating, receiving feedback and interpreting
- Evaluating - feasibility of ideas, performance, enabling self assessment

The Action Centred Leadership model therefore does not stand alone; it must be part of an integrated approach to managing and leading, and also which should include a strong emphasis on applying these principles through training. Adair also promotes a '50:50 rule' which he applies to various situations involving two possible influencers, e.g. the view that 50 per cent of motivation lies with the individual and 50 per cent comes from external factors, among them leadership from another. This contradicts most of the motivation gurus who assert that most motivation is from within the individual. He also suggests that 50 per cent of team building success comes from the team and 50 per cent from the leader.

Adair is an example of how management thinking changes and becomes more sophisticated over time, and in response to the development of previous management thinking. Personally I have great respect for Adair's work - it's far more accessible and relevant than much of the traditional previous gurus' thinking - it's holistic as well - you can see how it works easily in a multi-dimensional way, and above all believe it gets right to the heart of the leadership role, which explains very clearly why some succeed and others do not.

Use of John Adair's Action-centred Leadership Ideas, Theories and Diagram

Where you refer to John Adair's ideas about Action-Centred Leadership in teaching, training, coaching and learning please ensure you always attribute the concept and diagram to John Adair. This will help preserve the integrity and origins of his work. For general training, teaching and learning purposes you can of course refer to Adair's ideas and reproduce the three circles diagram, although when doing so please ensure you include the fact that the three circles is a trademark belonging to John Adair. This free usage includes normal educational 'fair use' such as:

- education of students in colleges and universities
- students' assignments and essays about management theories, etc
- reference to Adair's theory and the Action Centred Leadership diagram in management training courses (flip-charts, PowerPoint, notes, etc)
- review, critique and comparison with other ideas and theories within management training and education
- printing this webpage to use and/or copy as handouts, or cutting and pasting extracts for your own training materials (for non-commercial teaching only - NB, if you seek to include Adair-related material in commercial training delivery for profit, then you should seek permission from the Adair Leadership Foundation via the link below)

As ever please show the proper attributions, ownership and origins of the ideas in such usage. As with many of the pages on this website, this section on Adair's Action-Centred Leadership is a summary interpretation and an introduction to the ideas. If you want to find out more about John Adair's work, to explore his theories in more depth, or to use his ideas for publishing or commercial training programme design and delivery, you must seek permission and/or licence to do so, which can be pursued via John Adair's website, where there are good people able to help you.

Frederick Herzberg's Motivation and Hygiene Factors

Frederick Herzberg (1923-2000), clinical psychologist and pioneer of 'job enrichment', is regarded as one of the great original thinkers in management and motivational theory. Frederick I Herzberg was born in Massachusetts on April 18, 1923. His undergraduate work was at the City College of New York, followed by graduate degrees at the University of Pittsburgh. Herzberg was later Professor of Management at Case Western Reserve University, where he established the Department of Industrial Mental Health. He moved to the University of Utah's College of Business in 1972, where he was also Professor of Management. He died at Salt Lake City, January 18, 2000.

Frederick Herzberg's book 'The Motivation to Work', written with research colleagues Bernard Mausner and Barbara Bloch Snyderman in 1959, first established his theories about motivation in the workplace. Herzberg's survey work, originally on 200 Pittsburgh engineers and accountants remains a fundamentally important reference in motivational study. While the study involved only 200 people, Herzberg's considerable preparatory investigations, and the design of the research itself, enabled Herzberg and his colleagues to gather and analyse an extremely sophisticated level of data.

Herzberg's research used a pioneering approach, based on open questioning and very few assumptions, to gather and analyse details of 'critical incidents' as recalled by the survey respondents. He first used this methodology during his doctoral studies at the University of Pittsburgh with John Flanagan (later Director at the American Institute for Research), who developed the Critical Incident method in the selection of Army Air Corps personnel during the Second World War. Herzberg's clever open interviewing method gleaned far more meaningful results than the conventional practice of asking closed (basically yes/no) or multiple-choice or extent-based questions, which assume or prompt a particular type of response, and which incidentally remain the most popular and convenient style of surveying even today - especially among those having a particular agenda or publicity aim.

Herzberg also prepared intensively prior to his 1959 study - not least by scrutinizing and comparing the results and methodologies of all 155 previous research studies into job attitudes carried out between 1920 and 1954. The level of preparation, plus the 'critical incident' aspect and the depth of care and analysis during the 1959 project, helped make Herzberg's study such a powerful and sophisticated piece of work. Herzberg expanded his motivation-hygiene theory in his subsequent books: Work and the Nature of Man (1966); The Managerial Choice (1982); and Herzberg on Motivation (1983). Significantly, Herzberg commented in 1984, twenty-five years after his theory was first published: "The original study has produced more replications than any other research in the history of industrial and organizational psychology." (Source: Institute for Scientific Information) The absence of any serious challenge to Herzberg's theory continues effectively to validate it.

Hertzberg's Main Theory and Its Significance

Herzberg was the first to show that satisfaction and dissatisfaction at work nearly always arose from different factors, and were not simply opposing reactions to the same factors, as had always previously been (and still now by the unenlightened) believed. In 1959 Herzberg wrote the following useful little phrase, which helps explain this fundamental part of his theory, i.e., that the factors which motivate people at work are different to and not simply the opposite of the factors which cause dissatisfaction: "We can expand ... by stating that the *job satisfiers* deal with the *factors involved in doing the job,* whereas the *job dissatisfiers* deal with the *factors which define the job context.*" For graphical presentation of this principle, see the Herzberg hygiene factors and motivators graph diagram (revised April 2008), and the Herzberg diagram rocket and launch pad analogy diagram, (both are PDF files). The rocket analogy diagram, which incidentally is my own interpretation and not Herzberg's, is also available as a doc file and a PowerPoint slide: Herzberg rocket diagram doc (MSWord) format, and Herzberg rocket diagram ppt (MSPowerpoint) format. The graph diagram is also available in MSPowerpoint slide format: Herzberg's hygiene factors and motivators graph diagram ppt slide format.

The 2008 graph diagram is based on the total percentages of 'First-Level' factors arising in Herzberg's 1959 research of high and low attitude events among 200 engineers and accountants, encompassing short and long duration feelings. While Herzberg's overall conclusions were clear and consistent, the statistics from Herzberg's study can be interpreted in many different ways in their finer details, because of the depth and layering of Herzberg's survey methodology and analysis. For full details of the Herzberg study figures, and to fully appreciate the complexity and subtlety of his findings, see Herzberg's book The Motivation to Work. In addition to being really interesting and relevant to modern times, the book contains many tables of statistics and analysis, structured differently and extensively according to the variables that Herzberg considered to be important, for example, including the obvious main perspectives:

- high and low attitude (basically satisfaction and dissatisfaction, also defined as motivators and hygiene's or hygiene factors)
- short and long term duration of feelings (of high/low attitude effect)
- first and second level factors (i.e., main causal factors, and secondary factors deriving from the main stimulus, identified by further probing during interviews)
- the interrelationship of factors

These different perspectives obviously provided (and still provide) endless ways to analyse and present the results, although as stated already the main conclusions remain consistent. Incidentally, the 2008 revised graph diagram replaces the previous Herzberg factors diagram 2003 version, which I based on an interpretation of Herzberg's work by BACIE (British Association for Industrial and Commercial Education), appearing in their Handbook of Management Training Exercises published in 1978. BACIE referenced Herzberg's book Work and the Nature of Man, Staples Press 1966, but the root statistics and study are found in The Motivation to Work, 1959. I am unclear exactly how BACIE arrived at their figures reflected in the 2003 diagram, and it remains on this website mainly because it featured here for so long. If you use it please ensure you explain the background suitably. I am sure there are very many graphical interpretations of Herzberg's study results, which for the reasons explained will probably vary somewhat in the detail, although probably not too much in overall impression.

The purpose of the diagram (either version) is to illustrate how Herzberg's research showed that certain factors truly motivate ('motivators'), whereas others tended to lead to dissatisfaction ('hygiene factors'). According to Herzberg, Man has two sets of needs; one as an animal to avoid pain, and two as a human being to grow psychologically. He illustrated this also through Biblical example: Adam after his expulsion from Eden having the need for food, warmth, shelter, safety, etc., - the 'hygiene' needs; and Abraham, capable and achieving great things through self-development - the 'motivational' needs. Hertzberg's ideas relate strongly to modern ethical management and social responsibility. Many decades ago Herzberg, like Maslow, understood well and attempted to teach the ethical management principles that many leaders today, typically in businesses and organisations that lack humanity, still struggle to grasp. In this respect Herzberg's concepts are just as relevant now as when he first suggested them, except that the implications of responsibility, fairness, justice and compassion in business are now global.

Although Herzberg is most noted for his famous 'hygiene' and motivational factors theory, he was essentially concerned with people's well-being at work. Underpinning his theories and academic teachings, he was basically attempting to bring more humanity and caring into the workplace. He and others like him did not develop their theories to be used as 'motivational tools' purely to improve organisational performance. They sought instead primarily to explain how to manage people properly, for the good of all people at work. Herzberg's research proved that people will strive to achieve 'hygiene' needs because they are unhappy without them, but once satisfied the effect soon wears off - satisfaction is temporary. Then as now, poorly managed organisations fail to understand that people are not 'motivated' by addressing 'hygiene' needs. People are only truly motivated by enabling them to reach for and satisfy the factors that Herzberg identified as real motivators, such as achievement, advancement, development, etc., which represent a far deeper level of meaning and fulfillment. Examples of Herzberg's 'hygiene' needs (or maintenance factors) in the workplace are:

- policy
- relationship with supervisor
- work conditions
- salary
- company car
- status
- security
- relationship with subordinates
- personal life

Herzberg's research identified that true motivators were other completely different factors, notably:

- achievement

- recognition
- work itself
- responsibility
- advancement

N.B. Herzberg identified a specific category within the study responses which he called 'possibility of growth'. This arose in relatively few cases within the study and was not considered a major factor by Herzberg. Where referring to 'growth' or 'personal growth' in terms of Herzberg's primary motivators, 'growth' should be seen as an aspect of advancement, and not confused with the different matter of 'possibility of growth'.

To what Extent is Money a Motivator?

This question commonly arises when considering Herzberg's research and theories, so it's appropriate to include it here. Herzberg addressed money particularly (referring specifically to 'salary' in his study and analysis). Herzberg acknowledged the complexity of the salary issue (money, earnings, etc), and concluded that money is not a motivator in the way that the primary motivators are, such as achievement and recognition. "It [salary] appears as frequently in the high sequences ['sequences' refers to events causing high or low attitude feelings recalled by interviewees in the study] as it does in the low sequences... however... we find that in the lows [events leading to dissatisfaction], salary is found almost three times as often in the long-range as in the short-range attitude changes..." (There was no such bias towards the more important long-range feelings in the high attitude events.)

And about the interrelation of salary and other factors: "... when salary occurred as a factor in the lows (causes of dissatisfaction) it revolved around the unfairness of the wage system within the company... It was the system of salary administration that was being described... [or] it concerned an advancement that was not accompanied by a salary increase... In contrast to this, salary was mentioned in the high stories (events causing satisfaction) as something that went along with a person's achievement on the job. It was a form of recognition; it meant more than money; it meant a job well done; it meant that the individual was progressing in his work..." And Herzberg concluded about salary (i.e., money, earnings, etc): "*Viewed within the context of the sequences of events, salary as a factor belongs more in the group that defines the job situation and is primarily a dissatisfied.*"

- Many people argue nevertheless that money is a primary motivator.
- For most people money is not a motivator - despite what they might think and say.
- For *all people there are bigger more sustaining motivators than* money.

Surveys and research studies repeatedly show that other factors motivate more than money. Examples appear in the newspapers and in other information resources every week. For instance, a survey by Development Dimensions International published in the UK Times newspaper in 2004 interviewed 1,000 staff from companies employing more than 500 workers, and found many to be bored, lacking commitment and looking for a new job. Pay actually came fifth in the reasons people gave for leaving their jobs. The main reasons were lack of stimulus jobs and no opportunity for advancement - classic Herzberg motivators - 43 per cent left for better promotion chances, 28 per cent for more challenging work; 23 per cent for a more exciting place to work; and 21 per cent and more varied work. Lots of other evidence is found in life, wherever you care to look. Consider what happens when people win big lottery prize winners. While many of course give up their 'daily grind' jobs, some do not. They wisely recognize that their work is part of their purpose and life-balance.

Others who give up their jobs do so to buy or start and run their own businesses. They are pursuing their dream to achieve something special for them, whatever that might be. And whatever it means to them, the motivation is not to make money, otherwise why don't they just keep hold of what they've got? Why risk it on a project that will involve lots of effort and personal commitment? Of course the reason they invest in a new business venture is that pursuing this sort of plan is where the real motivators are found - achievement, responsibility, advancement, etc. not money. The people who are always the unhappy are those who focus on spending their money. The lottery prize-winners who give up work and pursue material and lifestyle pleasures soon find that life becomes empty and meaningless. Money, and spending it, is not enough to sustain the human spirit. We exist for more. Money is certainly important, and a personal driver, if you lack enough for a decent civilized existence, or you are striving for a house or a holiday, but beyond this, money is not for the vast majority of people a sustainable motivator in itself.

Douglas McGregor's XY Theory, managing an X Theory boss, and William Ouchi's Theory Z

Douglas McGregor, an American social psychologist, proposed his famous X-Y theory in his 1960 book 'The Human Side Of Enterprise'. Theory *x* and theory *y* are still referred to commonly in the field of management and motivation, and whilst more recent studies have questioned the rigidity of the model, Mcgregor's X-Y Theory remains a valid basic principle from which to develop positive management style and techniques. McGregor's XY Theory remains central to organizational development, and to improving organizational culture. McGregor's X-Y theory is a salutary and simple reminder of the natural rules for managing people, which under the pressure of day-to-day business are all too easily forgotten. McGregor maintained that there are two fundamental approaches to managing people. Many managers tend towards theory *x*, and generally get poor results. Enlightened managers use theory *y*, which produces better performance and results, and allows people to grow and develop.

Theory x ('authoritarian management' style)

- The average person dislikes work and will avoid it he/she can.
- Therefore most people must be forced with the threat of punishment to work towards organisational objectives.
- The average person prefers to be directed; to avoid responsibility; is relatively unambitious, and wants security above all else.

Theory y ('participative management' style)

- Effort in work is as natural as work and play.
- People will apply self-control and self-direction in the pursuit of organisational objectives, without external control or the threat of punishment.
- Commitment to objectives is a function of rewards associated with their achievement.
- People usually accept and often seek responsibility.
- The capacity to use a high degree of imagination, ingenuity and creativity in solving organisational problems is widely, not narrowly, distributed in the population.
- In industry the intellectual potential of the average person is only partly utilised.

Tools for Teaching, Understanding and Evaluating by Theory Factors

The XY Theory diagram and measurement tool below (PDF and doc versions) are adaptations of McGregor's ideas for modern organizations, management and work. They were not created by McGregor. I developed them to help understanding and application of McGregor's XY Theory concept. The test is a simple reflective tool, not a scientifically validated instrument; it's a learning aid and broad indicator. Please use it as such.

Characteristics of the x Theory Manager

Perhaps the most noticeable aspects of McGregor's XY Theory - and the easiest to illustrate - are found in the behaviours of autocratic managers and organizations which use autocratic management styles. What are the characteristics of a Theory X manager? Typically some, most or all of these:

- results-driven and deadline-driven, to the exclusion of everything else
- intolerant
- issues deadlines and ultimatums
- distant and detached
- aloof and arrogant
- elitist
- short temper
- shouts
- issues instructions, directions, edicts
- issues threats to make people follow instructions
- demands, never asks
- does not participate
- does not team-build
- unconcerned about staff welfare, or morale
- proud, sometimes to the point of self-destruction
- one-way communicator
- poor listener

- fundamentally insecure and possibly neurotic
- anti-social
- vengeful and recriminatory
- does not thank or praise
- withholds rewards, and suppresses pay and remunerations levels
- scrutinises expenditure to the point of false economy
- seeks culprits for failures or shortfalls
- seeks to apportion blame instead of focusing on learning from the experience and preventing recurrence
- does not invite or welcome suggestions
- takes criticism badly and likely to retaliate if from below or peer group
- poor at proper delegating - but believes they delegate well
- thinks giving orders is delegating
- holds on to responsibility but shifts accountability to subordinates
- relatively unconcerned with investing in anything to gain future improvements
- unhappy

How to Manage Upwards—Managing your X Theory Boss

Working for an X theory boss isn't easy - some extreme X theory managers make extremely unpleasant managers, but there are ways of managing these people upwards. Avoiding confrontation (unless you are genuinely being bullied, which is a different matter) and delivering results are the key tactics.

- Theory X managers (or indeed theory Y managers displaying theory X behaviour) are primarily results oriented - so orientate your own discussions and dealings with them around results - i.e. what you can deliver and when.

- Theory X managers are facts and figures oriented - so cut out the incidentals, be able to measure and substantiate anything you say and do for them, especially reporting on results and activities.
- Theory X managers generally don't understand or have an interest in the human issues, so don't try to appeal to their sense of humanity or morality. Set your own objectives to meet their organisational aims and agree these with the managers; be seen to be self-starting, self-motivating, self-disciplined and well-organised - the more the X theory manager sees you are managing yourself and producing results, the less they'll feel the need to do it for you.
- Always deliver your commitments and promises. If you are given an unrealistic task and/or deadline state the reasons why it's not realistic, but be very sure of your ground, don't be negative; be constructive as to how the overall aim can be achieved in a way that you know you can deliver.
- Stand up for yourself, but constructively - avoid confrontation. Never threaten or go over their heads if you are dissatisfied or you'll be in big trouble afterwards and life will be a lot more difficult.
- If an X theory boss tells you how to do things in ways that are not comfortable or right for you, then don't questioning the process, simply confirm the end-result that is required, and check that it's okay to 'streamline the process' or 'get things done more efficiently' if the chance arises - they'll normally agree to this, which effectively gives you control over the 'how', provided you deliver the 'what' and 'when'.

And this is really the essence of managing upwards X theory managers - focus and get agreement on the results and deadlines - if you consistently deliver, you'll increasingly be given more leeway on how you go about the tasks, which amounts to more freedom. Be aware also that many X theory managers are forced to be X theory by the short-term demands of the organisation and their own superiors - an X theory manager is usually someone with their own problems, so try not to give them any more.

Theory z - William ouchi

First things first - Theory Z is not a Mcgregor idea and as such is not Mcgregor's extension of his XY theory. Theory Z was developed by not by Mcgregor, but by William Ouchi, in his book 1981 'Theory Z: How American management can meet the Japanese Challenge'. William Ouchi is professor of management at UCLA, Los Angeles, and a board member of several large US organisations. Theory Z is often referred to as the 'Japanese' management style, which is essentially what it is. It's interesting that Ouchi chose to name his model 'Theory Z', which apart from anything else tends to give the impression that it's a Mcgregor idea. One wonders if the idea was not considered strong enough to stand alone with a completely new name... Nevertheless, Theory Z essentially advocates a combination of all that's best about theory Y and modern Japanese management, which places a large amount of freedom and trusts with workers, and assumes that workers have a strong loyalty and interest in team-working and the organisation.

Theory Z also places more reliance on the attitude and responsibilities of the workers, whereas Mcgregor's XY theory is mainly focused on management and motivation from the manager's and organisation's perspective. There is no doubt that Ouchi's Theory Z model offers excellent ideas, albeit it lacking the simple elegance of Mcgregor's model, which let's face it, thousands of organisations and managers around the world have still yet to embrace. For this reason, Theory Z may for some be like trying to manage the kitchen at the Ritz before mastering the ability to cook a decent fried breakfast.

To develop your understanding of McGregor's X-Y Theory, complete the free McGregor XY Theory Test (PDF), or doc version, which indicates whether your organisation is more Theory-X or Theory-Y, as well as indicating your own (or the particular individual's) preference to be managed by X or Y style. The test is a simple reflective tool, not a scientifically validated instrument, designed to give a broad indication of XY Theory tendencies and to aid understanding of the model. The free XY Theory diagram (PDF) or doc version, is helpful for teaching and training, presentations and project work, and is adapted from McGregor's ideas so as to convey simply and quickly the essence of the concept.

Stacey Adams—Equity Theory on Job Motivation

John Stacey Adams, a workplace and behavioural psychologist, put forward his Equity Theory on job motivation in 1963. There are similarities with Charles Handy's extension and interpretation of previous simpler theories of Maslow, Herzberg and other pioneers of workplace psychology, in that the theory acknowledges that subtle and variable factors affect each individual's assessment and perception of their relationship with their work, and thereby their employer. However, awareness and cognizance of the wider situation - and crucially *comparison* - feature more strongly in Equity Theory than in many other earlier motivational models.

The Adams' Equity Theory model therefore extends beyond the individual self, and incorporates influence and comparison of other people's situations - for example colleagues and friends - in forming a comparative view and awareness of Equity, which commonly manifests as a sense of what is fair. When people feel fairly or advantageously treated they are more likely to be motivated; when they feel unfairly treated they are highly prone to feelings of disaffection and demotivation. The way that people measure this sense of fairness is at the heart of Equity Theory. Equity, and thereby the motivational situation we might seek to assess using the model, is not dependent on the extent to which a person believes reward exceeds effort, nor even necessarily on the belief that reward exceeds effort at all. Rather, Equity, and the sense of fairness which commonly underpins motivation, is dependent on the comparison a person makes between his or here reward/investment ratio with the ratio enjoyed (or suffered) by others considered to be in a similar situation.

Adams' Equity Theory

Adams called personal *efforts* and *rewards* and other similar *'give and take'* issues at work respectively *'inputs'* and *'outputs'*. Inputs are logically what we give or put into our work. Outputs are everything we take out in return. These terms help emphasise that what people put into their work includes many factors besides working hours, and that what people receive from their work includes many things aside from money. Adams used the term *'referent' others* to describe *the reference points or people with whom we compare our own situation,* which is the *pivotal part of the theory.* Adams Equity Theory goes beyond - and is quite different from merely assessing effort and reward. Equity Theory adds a crucial additional perspective of comparison with 'referent' others (people we consider in a similar situation).

Equity theory thus helps explain why pay and conditions alone do not determine motivation. In terms of how the theory applies to work and management, we each seek a fair balance between what we put into our job and what we get out of it. But how do we decide what is a *fair* balance? The answer lies in Equity Theory. Importantly we arrive at our measure of fairness - Equity - by comparing our balance of effort and reward, and other factors of give and take - the ratio of input and output - with the balance or ratio enjoyed by other people, whom we deem to be relevant reference points or examples ('referent' others).

Crucially this means that Equity does not depend on our input-to-output ratio alone - it depends on our comparison between our ratio and the ratio of others. We form perceptions of what constitutes a fair ratio (a balance or trade) of inputs and outputs by comparing our own situation with other 'referents' (reference points or examples) in the market place as we see it. In practice this helps to explain why people are so strongly affected by the situations (and views and gossip) of colleagues, friends, partners etc., in establishing their own personal sense of fairness or equity in their work situations.

Adams' Equity Theory is therefore a far more complex and sophisticated motivational model than merely assessing effort (inputs) and reward (outputs). The actual sense of equity or fairness (or inequity or unfairness) within Equity Theory is arrived at only after incorporating a comparison between our own input and output ratio with the input and output ratios that we see or believe to be experienced or enjoyed by others in similar situations.

This comparative aspect of Equity Theory provides a far more fluid and dynamic appreciation of motivation than typically arises in motivational theories and models based on individual circumstance alone. For example, Equity Theory explains why people can be happy and motivated by their situation one day, and yet with no change to their terms and working conditions can be made very unhappy and demotivated, if they learn for example that a colleague (or worse an entire group) is enjoying a better reward-to-effort ratio. It also explains why giving one person a promotion or pay-rise can have a demotivating effect on others.

Note also, importantly, that what matters is the *ratio,* not the amount of effort or reward per se. This explains for example why and how full-time employees will compare their situations and input-to-output ratios with part-time colleagues, who very probably earn less, however it is the ratio of input-to-output - reward-to-effort - which counts, and if the part-timer is perceived to enjoy a more advantageous ratio, then so this will have a negative effect on the full-timer's sense of Equity, and with it, their personal motivation. Remember also that words like efforts and rewards, or work and pay, are an over-simplification - hence Adams' use of the terms inputs and outputs, which more aptly cover all aspects of what a person gives, sacrifices, tolerates, invests, etc., into their work situation, and all aspects of what a person receives and benefits from in their work and wider career, as they see it.

inputs	**equity** dependent on comparing own ratio of input/ output with ratios of 'referent' others	**outputs**
Inputs are typically: effort, loyalty, hard work, commitment, skill, ability, adaptability, flexibility, tolerance, determination, heart and soul, enthusiasm, trust in our boss and superiors, support of colleagues and subordinates, personal sacrifice, etc.	People need to feel that there is a fair balance between inputs and outputs. Crucially fairness is measured by comparing one's own balance or ratio between inputs and outputs, with the ratio enjoyed or endured by relevant ('referent') others.	Outputs are typically all financial rewards - pay, salary, expenses, perks, benefits, pension arrangements, bonus and commission - plus intangibles - recognition, reputation, praise and thanks, interest, responsibility, stimulus, travel, training, development, sense of achievement and advancement, promotion, etc.

If we feel are that inputs are *fairly* rewarded by outputs (the *fairness* benchmark being subjectively perceived from market norms and other comparable references) then generally we are happier in our work and more motivated to continue inputting at the same level. If we feel that our ratio of inputs to outputs is less beneficial than the ratio enjoyed by referent others, then we become demotivated in relation to our job and employer. Generally the extent of demotivation is proportional to the perceived disparity with other people or inequity, but for some people just the smallest indication of negative disparity between their situation and other people's is enough to cause massive disappointment and a feeling of considerable injustice, resulting in demotivation, or worse, open hostility. Some people reduce effort and application and become inwardly disgruntled, or outwardly difficult, recalcitrant or even disruptive. Other people seek to improve the outputs by making claims or demands for more reward, or seeking an alternative job.

Understanding Equity Theory - and especially its pivotal comparative aspect - helps managers and policy-makers to appreciate that while improving one person's terms and conditions can resolve that individual's demands (for a while), if the change is perceived by other people to upset the Equity of their own situations then the solution can easily generate far more problems than it attempted to fix. Equity Theory reminds us that people see themselves and crucially the way they are treated in terms of their surrounding environment, team, system, etc - not in isolation - and so they must be managed and treated accordingly.

A free fully detailed diagram similar to the image below explaining Adam's Equity Theory is available in various formats. When using or referring to the diagram emphasise that the calibration of the scales - the comparison of input/ output ratios - is the crucial aspect, not merely a judgement of whether rewards are appropriate for efforts:

This interpretation of Adams' Equity Theory was updated and improved in December 2007. The previous summary failed to emphasise the pivotal significance of the comparative aspect within the theory. Thanks NT for your guidance in making these improvements.

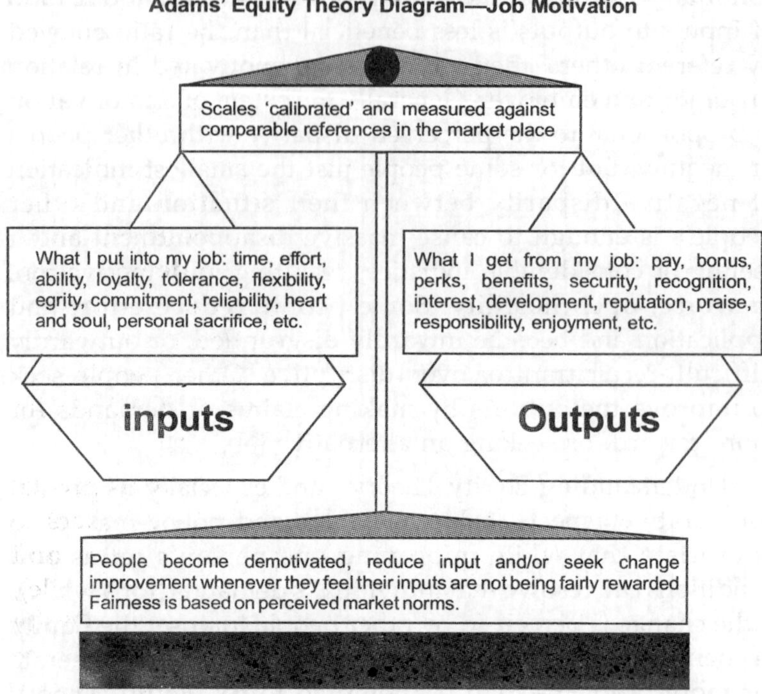

Erikson's Psychosocial Development Theory

Erikson's model of psychosocial development is a very significant, highly regarded and meaningful concept. Life is a serious of lessons and challenges which help us to grow. Erikson's wonderful theory helps to tell us why. The theory is helpful for child development and adults too. For the 'lite' version, here's a quick diagram and summary. Extra details follow the initial overview. For more information than appears on this page, read Erikson's books; he was an award-winning writer and this review does not convey the richness of Erikson's own explanations. It's also interesting to see how his ideas develop over time, perhaps aided by his own journey through the 'psychosocial crisis' stages model that underpinned his work. Erik Erikson first published his eight stage theory of human development in his 1950 book Childhood and Society. The chapter featuring the model was titled 'The Eight Ages of Man'. He expanded and refined his theory in later books and revisions, notably: Identity and the Life Cycle (1959); Insight and Responsibility (1964); The Life Cycle Completed: A Review (1982, revised 1996 by Joan Erikson); and Vital Involvement in Old Age (1989). Erikson's biography lists more books.

Various terms are used to describe Erikson's model, for example Erikson's biopsychosocial or bio-psycho-social theory (bio refers to biological, which in this context means life); Erikson's human development cycle or life cycle, and variations of these. All refer to the same eight stages psychosocial theory, it being Erikson's most distinct work and remarkable model. The word 'psychosocial' is Erikson's term, effectively from the words psychological (mind) and social (relationships).

Erikson believed that his psychosocial principle is genetically inevitable in shaping human development. It occurs in all people. He also referred to his theory as 'epigenesis' and the 'epigenetic principle', which signified the concept's relevance to evolution (past and future) and genetics. Erikson explained his use of the word 'epigenesis' thus: "...epic can mean 'above' in space as well as 'before' in time and in connection with genesis can well represent the space-time nature of all development..." (from Vital Involvement in Old Age, 1989). In Erikson's theory, Epigenetic therefore does not refer to individual genetic make-up and its influence on individual development. This was not central to Erikson's ideas. Erikson, like Freud, was largely concerned with how personality and behaviour is influenced after birth - not before birth - and especially during childhood. In the 'nature v nurture' (genes v experience) debate, Erikson was firmly focused on nurture and experie nce.

Erik Eriksson's Eight Stages of Psychosocial Development

Like other seminal concepts, Erikson's model is simple and elegant, yet very sophisticated. The theory is a basis for broad or complex discussion and analysis of personality and behaviour, and also for understanding and for facilitating personal development - of self and others. The main elements of the theory covered in this explanation are:

- Erikson theory overview—a diagram and concise explanation of the main features of model.
- The Freudian stages of psychosexual development, which influenced Erikson's approach to the psychosocial model.
- Erikson's 'psychosocial crises' (or crisis stages) - meanings and interpretations.
- 'Basic virtues' (basic strengths) - the potential positive outcomes arising from each of the crisis stages.
- 'Maladapations' and 'Malignancies' - potential negative outcomes (one or the other) arising from each crisis stage.
- Erikson terminology - variations and refinements to names and headings, etc.
- Erik Erikson biography (briefly)

N.B. This summary occasionally uses the terms 'positive' and 'negative' to identify the first or second factors in each crisis (e.g., Trust = positive; Mistrust = negative) however no crisis factor (disposition or emotional force - whatever you choose to call them - descriptions are quite tricky as even Erikson found) is actually wholly positive or wholly negative. Healthy personality development is based on a sensible balance between 'positive' and 'negative' dispositions at each crisis stage. Erikson didn't use the words positive and negative in this sense. He tended to use 'syntonic' and 'dystonic' to differentiate between the two sides of each crisis, which is why I occasionally use the more recognisable 'positive' and 'negative' terms, despite them being potentially misleading. You should also qualify your use of these terms if using them in relation to the crisis stages.

Eriksson's Psychosocial Theory—Summary Diagram

Here's a broad introduction to the main features of Erikson's model. Various people have produced different interpretations like this grid below. Erikson produced a few charts of his own too, from different perspectives, but he seems never to have produced a fully definitive matrix. To aid explanation and use of his theory he produced several perspectives in grid format, some of which he advocated be used as worksheets. He viewed his concept as an evolving work in progress. This summary attempts to show the main points of the Erikson psychosocial crisis theory of human development. More detail follows this overview.

The colours are merely to help presentation and do not signify any relationships between factors. This chart attempts to capture and present concisely the major elements of Erikson's theory, drawn from various Erikson books, diagrams and other references, including Childhood and Society (1950); Identity and the Life Cycle (1959); The Life Cycle Completed: A Review (1982, revised 1996 by Joan Erikson); and Vital Involvement in Old Age (1989). Erikson later suggested psychosexual stages 7 and 8, but they are not typically part of Freud's scheme which extended only to Puberty/Geniality. See Freud's psychosexual stages below.

Erik Eriksson's Psychosocial Theory Overview

Erikson's psychosocial theory is widely and highly regarded. As with any concept there are critics, but generally Erikson's theory is considered fundamentally significant. Erikson was a psychoanalyst and also a humanitarian. So his theory is useful far beyond psychoanalysis - it's useful for any application involving personal awareness and development -

Erikson's psychosocial crisis stages (syntonic v dystonic)	Freudian psycho-sexual stages	Life stage/relationship/ issues	basic virtue and second named strength (potential outcomes from each crisis)	maladaptation/ malignancy (potential negative outcome-one or the other-from unhelpful experience during each crisis)
1. Trust Mistrust	Oral	Infant/mother/feeding and being comforted, teething, sleeping	Hope and Drive	Sensory Distortion/ Withdrawal
2. Autonomy v Shame & Doubt	Anal	toddler/parents/bodily functions, toilet training, muscular control, walking	Will power and Self-Control	Impulsivity/ Compulsion
3. Initiative v Guilt	Phallic	preschool/family/exploration and discovery, adventure and play	Purpose and Direction	Ruthlessness/ Inhibition
4. Industry v Inferiority	Latency	schoolchild/school, teachers, friends, neighbourhood/ achievement and accomplishment	Competence and Method	Narrow Virtuosity/ Inertia
5. Identity v Role Confusion	Puberty and Genialty	adolescent/peers, groups, influences/ resolving identity and direction, becoming a grown-up	Fidelity and Devotion	Fanaticism/ Repudiatio
6. Intimacy v Isolation	(Geniality)	young adult/lovers, friends, work connections/ intimate relationships, work and social life	Love and Affiliation	Promiscuity/ Exclusivity
7. Generativist v Stagnation	n/a	mid-adult/children, community/ 'giving back', helping, contributing	Care and Production	Over extension/ Receptivity
8. Integrity v Despair	n/a	late adult/society, the world life/ meaning and pupose, life achievements	Wisdom and Renunciation	Presumption/ Disdain

of oneself or others. There is a strong, but not essential, Freudian element in Erikson's work and model. Fans of Freud will find the influence useful. People, who disagree with Freud, and especially his psychosexual theory, can ignore the Freudian aspect and still find Erikson's ideas useful. Erikson's theory stands alone and does not depend on Freud for its robustness and relevance.

Aside from Freudian psychoanalysis, Erikson developed his theory mainly from his extensive practical field research, initially with Native American communities, and then also from his clinical therapy work attached to leading mental health centres and universities. He actively pioneered psychoanalytical development from the late 1940's until the 1990's. Erikson's concept crucially incorporated *cultural and social aspects* into Freud's biological and sexually oriented theory. Erikson was able to do this because of his strong interest and compassion for people, especially young people, and also because his research was carried out among human societies far removed from the more inward-looking world of the psychoanalyst's couch, which was essentially Freud's approach.

This helps Erikson's eight stages theory to be a tremendously powerful model: it is very accessible and obviously relevant to modern life, from several different perspectives, for understanding and explaining how personality and behaviour develops in people. As such Erikson's theory is useful for teaching, parenting, self-awareness, managing and coaching, dealing with conflict, and generally for understanding self and others. Both Erikson and his wife Joan, who collaborated as psychoanalysts and writers, were passionately interested in childhood development, and its effects on adult society. Eriksons' work is as relevant today as when he first outlined his original theory, in fact given the modern pressures on society, family and relationships—and the quest for personal development and fulfillment—his ideas are probably more relevant now than ever.

Erikson's psychosocial theory basically asserts that people experience eight 'psychosocial crisis stages' which significantly affect each person's development and personality. Joan Erikson described a 'ninth' stage after Erik's death, but the eight stage model is most commonly referenced and is regarded as the standard. (Joan Erikson's work on the 'ninth stage' appears in her 1996 revisions to The Life Cycle Completed: A Review, and will in the future be summarised on this page.)

Erikson's theory refers to 'psychosocial crisis' (or psychosocial crises, being the plural). This term is an extension of Sigmund Freud's use of the word 'crisis', which represents internal emotional conflict. You might also describe this sort of crisis as an internal struggle or challenge which a person must negotiate and deal with in order to grow and develop. Erikson's 'psychosocial' term is derived from the two source words - namely *psychological* (or the root, 'psycho' relating to the mind, brain, personality, etc) and *social* (external relationships and environment), both at the heart of Erikson's theory. Occasionally you'll see the term extended to biopsychosocial, in which bio refers to life, as in *biological.*

Each stage involves a crisis of two opposing emotional forces. A helpful term used by Erikson for these opposing forces is 'contrary dispositions'. Each crisis stage relates to a corresponding life stage and its inherent challenges. Erikson used the words 'syntonic' for the first-listed 'positive' disposition in each crisis (e.g., Trust) and 'dystonic' for the second-listed 'negative' disposition (e.g., Mistrust). To signify the opposing or conflicting relationship between each pair of forces or dispositions Erikson connected them with the word 'versus', which he abbreviated to 'v'. (Versus is Latin, meaning turned towards or against.) The actual definitions of the syntonic and dystonic words (see Erikson's terminology below) are mainly irrelevant unless you have a passion for the detailed history of Erikson's ideas.

Successfully passing through each crisis involves 'achieving' a *healthy ratio or balance* between the two opposing dispositions that represent each crisis. For example a healthy balance at crisis stage one (Trust v Mistrust) might be described as experiencing and growing through the crisis 'Trust' (of people, life and one's future development) and also experiencing and growing a suitable capacity for 'Mistrust' where appropriate, so as not to be hopelessly unrealistic or gullible, nor to be mistrustful of everything. Or experiencing and growing through stage two (Autonomy v Shame & Doubt) to be essentially 'Autonomous' (to be one's own person and not a mindless or quivering follower) but to have sufficient capacity for 'Shame and Doubt', so as to be free-thinking and independent, while also being ethical and considerate and responsible, etc.

Erikson called these successful balanced outcomes 'Basic Virtues' or 'Basic Strengths'. He identified one particular word to represent the fundamental strength gained at each stage, which appear commonly in Erikson's diagrams and written theory, and other explanations of his work. Erikson also identified a second supporting 'strength' word at each stage, which along with the basic virtue emphasised the main healthy outcome at each stage, and helped convey simple meaning in summaries and charts. Examples of basic virtues and supporting strengths words are 'Hope and Drive' (from stage one, Trust v Mistrust) and 'Willpower and Self-Control' (from stage two, Autonomy v Shame & Doubt). It's very useful however to gain a more detailed understanding of the meaning behind these words because although Erikson's choice these words is very clever, and the words are very symbolic, using just one or two words alone is not adequate for truly conveying the depth of the theory, and particularly the emotional and behavioural strengths that arise from healthy progression through each crisis. More detail about basic virtues and strengths is in the Basic Virtues section.

Erikson was sparing in his use of the word 'achieve' in the context of successful outcomes, because it implied gaining something clear-cut and permanent. Psychosocial development is not clear-cut and is not irreversible: any previous crisis can effectively revisit anyone, albeit in a different guise, with successful or unsuccessful results. This perhaps helps explain how 'high achievers' can fall from grace, and how 'hopeless failures' can ultimately achieve great things. No-one should become complacent, and there is hope for us all. Later in his life Erikson was keen to warn against interpreting his theory into an 'achievement scale', in which the crisis stages represent single safe achievement or target of the extreme 'positive' option, secured once and for ever. Erikson said (in Identity and the Life Cycle): "...What the child acquires at a given stage is a certain *ratio* between the positive and negative, which if the balance is toward the positive, will help him to meet later crises with a better chance for unimpaired total development..."

He continued (in rather complicated language, hence paraphrasing) that at no stage can a 'goodness' be achieved which is impervious to new conflicts, and that to believe so is dangerous and inept. The crisis stages are not sharply defined steps. Elements tend to overlap and mingle from one stage to the next and to the preceding stages. It's a broad framework and concept, not a mathematical formula which replicates precisely across all people and situations. Erikson was keen to point out that the transition between stages is 'overlapping'. Crisis stages connect with each other like interlaced fingers, not like a series of neatly stacked boxes. People don't suddenly wake up one morning and be in a new life stage. Changes don't happen in regimented clear-cut steps. Changes are graduated, mixed-together and organic. In this respect the 'feel' of the model is similar to other flexible human development frameworks (for example, Elisabeth Kübler-Ross's 'Grief Cycle', and Maslow's Hierarchy of Needs).

Where a person passes *unsuccessfully* through a psychosocial crisis stage they develop a tendency towards one or other of the opposing forces (either to the syntonic or the dystonic, in Erikson's language), which then becomes a behavioural tendency, or even a mental problem. In crude terms we might call this 'baggage' or a 'hang-up', although perhaps avoid such terms in serious work. I use them here to illustrate that Erikson's ideas are very much related to real life and the way ordinary people think and wonder about things.Erikson called an extreme tendency towards the syntonic (first disposition) a 'maladapation', and he identified specific words to represent the maladapation at each stage. He called an extreme tendency towards the dystonic (second disposition) a 'malignancy', and again he identified specific words to represent the malignancy at each stage. More under 'Maladapations' and 'Malignancies'.

Erikson emphasised the significance of and 'mutuality' and 'generativity' in his theory. The terms are linked. Mutuality reflects the effect of generations on each other, especially among families, and particularly between parents and children and grandchildren. Everyone potentially affects everyone else's experiences as they pass through the different crisis stages. Generativity, actually a named disposition within one of the crisis stages (Generativity v Stagnation, stage seven), reflects the significant relationship between adults and the best interests of children - one's own children, and in a way everyone else's children - the next generation, and all following generations.

Generations affect each other. A parent obviously affects the child's psychosocial development, but in turn the parent's psychosocial development is affected by their experience of dealing with the child and the pressures produced. Same for grandparents. Again this helps explain why as parents (or teachers or siblings or grandparents) we can often struggle to deal well with a young person when it's as much as we can do to deal with our own emotional challenges. In some ways the development actually peaks at stage seven, since stage eight is more about taking stock and coming to terms with how one has made use of life, and ideally preparing to leave it feeling at peace. The perspective of giving and making a positive difference for future generation echoes Erikson's humanitarian philosophy, and it's this perhaps more than anything else that enabled him to develop such a powerful concept.

Eriksson's Psychosocial Theory in more Detail

Erikson's psychosocial theory of the 'eight stages of human development' drew from and extended the ideas of Sigmund Freud and Freud's daughter Anna Freud, and particularly the four (or five, depending on interpretation) Freudian stages of development, known as Freud's psychosexual stages or Freud's sexual theory. These concepts are fundamental to Freudian thinking and are outlined below in basic terms relating to Erikson's psychosocial stages. Freud's concepts, while influential on Erikson, are not however fundamental to Erikson's theory, which stands up perfectly well in its own right. It is not necessary therefore to understand or agree with Freud's ideas in order to appreciate and use Erikson's theory. If you naturally relate to Freud's ideas fine, otherwise leave them to one side.

Part of Erikson's appeal is that he built on Freud's ideas in a socially meaningful and accessible way - and in a way that did not wholly rely on adherence to fundamental Freudian thinking. Some of Freud's theories by their nature tend attract a lot of attention and criticism - sex, breasts, genitals, and bodily functions generally do - and if you are distracted or put off by these references then ignore them, because they are not crucial for understanding and using Erikson's model.

Freud's Psychosexual Stages—Overview

Age guide is a broad approximation, hence the overlaps. The stages happen in this sequence, but not to a fixed timetable.

Freudian psychosexual stages – overview	Erikson's psychosocial crisis stages	age guide
1	2	3
1. Oral Stage - Feeding, crying, teething, biting, thumb-sucking, weaning - the mouth and the breast are the centre of all experience. The infant's actual experiences and attachments to mum (or maternal equivalent) through this stage have a fundamental effect on the unconscious mind and thereby on deeply rooted feelings, which along with the next two stages affect all sorts of behaviours and (sexually powered) drives and aims - Freud's 'libido' - and preferences in later life.	1. Trust v Mistrust	0-1½ yrs, baby, birth to walking
2. Anal Stage - It's a lot to do with pooh - 'holding on' or 'letting go' - the pleasure and control. Is it dirty? Is it okay? Bodily expulsions are the centre of the world, and the pivot around which early character is formed. Am I pleasing my mum and dad? Are they making me feel good or bad about my bottom? Am I okay or naughty? Again the young child's actual experiences through this stage have a deep effect on the unconscious and behaviours and preferences in later life.	2. Autonomy v Shame and Doubt	1-3 yrs, toddler, toilet training
3. Phallic Stage - Phallic is not restricted to boys. This stage is focused on resolving reproductive issues. This is a sort of dry run before the real game starts in adolescence. Where do babies come from? Can I have a baby? Why has dad got a willy and I've not? Why have I got a willy and	3. Initiative v Guilt	3-6 yrs, pre-school, nursery

1	2	3
mum hasn't? Why do they tell me off for touching my bits and pieces down there? (Boys) I'm going to marry mum (and maybe kill dad). (Girls) I'm in love with my dad. Oedipus Complex, Penis envy, Castration Anxiety, etc. "If you touch yourself down there it'll fall off/heal up.." Inevitably once more, experiences in this stage have a profound effect on feelings and behaviour and libido in later life. If you want to know more about all this I recommend you read about Freud, not Erikson, and I repeat that understanding Freud's psychosexual theory is not required for understanding and using Erikson's concepts.		•
4. Latency Stage - Sexual dormancy or repression. The focus is on learning, skills, schoolwork. This is actually not a psychosexual stage because basically normally nothing formative happens sexually. Experiences, fears and conditioning from the previous stages have already shaped many of the child's feelings and attitudes and these will re-surface in the next stage.	4. Industry v Inferiority	5-12 yrs, early school
5. Genital stage - Puberty in other words. Glandular, hormonal, and physical changes in the adolescent child's body cause a resurgence of sexual thoughts, feelings and behaviours. Boys start treating their mothers like woman-servants and challenge their fathers (Freud's 'Oedipus'). Girls flirt with their	5. Identity v Role Confusion	11-18 yrs, puberty, teens earlier for girls

1	2	3
fathers and argue with their mums (Freud's 'Electra'). All become highly agitated if away from a mirror for more than half an hour (Freud's Narcissus or Narcissism). Dating and fondling quickly push schoolwork and sports (and anything else encouraged by parents and figures of authority) into second place. Basically everyone is in turmoil and it's mostly to do with growing up, which entails more sexual undercurrents than parents would ever believe, even though these same parents went through exactly the same struggles themselves just a few years before. It's a wonder anyone ever makes it to adulthood, but of course they do, and mostly it's all perfectly normal.This is the final Freudian psychosexual stage. Erikson's model, which from the start offers a different and more socially oriented perspective, continues through to old age, and re-interprets Freudian sexual theory into the adult life stages equating to Erikson's crisis stages. This incorporation of Freudian sexual stages into the adult crisis stages is not especially significant.		
Arguably no direct equivalent Freudian stage, although as from Identity and the Life Cycle (1969) Erikson clearly separated Puberty and Genitality (Freud's Genital stage) , and related each respectively to Identity v Role Confusion, and Intimacy v Isolation.	6. Intimacy v Isolation	18-40, courting, early parenthood

1	2	3
No direct equivalent Freudian stage, although Erikson later interpreted this as being a psychosexual stage of 'Procreativity'.	7. Generativity v Stagnation	30-65, middle age, parenting
Again no direct equivalent Freudian stage. Erikson later called this the psychosexual stage of 'Generalization of Sensual Modes'.	8. Integrity v Despair	50+, old age, grand parents

N.B. This is a quick light overview of Freud's sexual theory and where it equates to Erikson's crisis stages. It's not meant to be a serious detailed analysis of Freud's psychosexual ideas. That said, I'm open to suggestions from any Freud experts out there who would like to offer improved (quick, easy, down-to-earth) pointers to the Freudian psychosexual theory.

Eriksson's Eight Psychosocial Crisis Stages

Here's a more detailed interpretation of Erikson's psychosocial crisis stages. Remember age range is just a very rough guide, especially through the later levels when parenthood timing and influences vary. Hence the overlap between the ages ranges in the interpretation below. Interpretations of age range vary among writers and academics. Erikson intentionally did not stipulate clear fixed age stages, and it's impossible for anyone to do so.

Below is a reminder of the crisis stages, using the crisis terminology of the original 1950 model aside from the shorter terminology that Erikson later preferred for stages one and eight. The 'Life Stage' names were suggested in later writings by Erikson and did not appear so clearly in the 1950 model. Age range and other descriptions are general interpretations and were not shown specifically like this by Erikson. Erikson's main terminology changes are explained below. Crisis stages are driven by physical and sexual growth, which then prompts the life issues which create the crises. The crises are therefore not driven by age precisely. Erikson never showed precise ages, and I prefer to state wider age ranges than many other common interpretations. The final three (adult) stages happen at particularly variable ages.

It's worth noting also that these days there's a lot more 'life' and complexity in the final (old age) stage than when the eight stages were originally outlined, which no doubt fuelled Joan Erikson's ideas on a 'ninth stage' after Erik's death.

Eriksson's Eight Psychosocial Stages

Psychosocial Crisis Stage	Life Stage	age range, other descriptions
1. Trust v Mistrust	Infancy	0-1½ yrs, baby, birth to walking
2. Autonomy v Shame and Doubt	Early Childhood	1-3 yrs, toddler, toilet training
3. Initiative v Guilt	Play Age	3-6 yrs, pre-school, nursery
4. Industry v Inferiority	School Age	5-12 yrs, early school
5. Identity v Role Confusion	Adolescence	9-18 yrs, puberty, teens*
6. Intimacy v Isolation	Young Adult	18-40, courting, early parenthood
7. Generativity v Stagnation	Adulthood	30-65, middle age, parenting
8. Integrity v Despair	Mature Age	50+, old age, grandparents

* Other interpretations of the Adolescence stage commonly suggest stage 5 begins around 12 years of age. This is reasonable for most boys, but given that Erikson and Freud cite the onset of puberty as the start of this stage, stage 5 can begin for girls as early as age nine. Erikson's psychosocial

theory essentially states that each person experiences eight *'psychosocial crises'* (internal conflicts linked to life's key stages) which help to define his or her growth and personality. People experience these 'psychosocial crisis' stages in a fixed sequence, but timings vary according to people and circumstances.

This is why the stages and the model are represented primarily by the names of the crises or emotional conflicts themselves (e.g., Trust v Mistrust) rather than strict age or life stage definitions. Age and life stages do feature in the model, but as related rather than pivotal factors, and age ranges are increasingly variable as the stages unfold. Each of the eight 'psychosocial crises' is characterised by a conflict between two opposing positions or attitudes (or dispositions or emotional forces). Erikson never really settled on a firm recognisable description for the two components of each crisis, although in later works the first disposition is formally referred to as the 'Adaptive Strength'. He also used the terms 'syntonic' and 'dystonic' for respectively the first and second dispositions in each crisis, but not surprisingly these esoteric words never featured strongly in interpretations of Erikson's terminology, and their usual meanings are not very helpful in understanding what Erikson meant in this context.

The difficulty in 'labeling' the first and second dispositions in each crisis is a reflection that neither is actually wholly good or bad, or wholly positive or negative. The first disposition is certainly the preferable tendency, but an ideal outcome is achieved only when it is counter-balanced with a degree of the second disposition. Successful development through each crisis is requires a balance and ratio between the two dispositions, not total adoption of the apparent 'positive' disposition, which if happens can produce almost as much difficulty as a strong or undiluted tendency towards the second 'negative' disposition. Some of the crisis stages are easier to understand than others. Each stage contains far more meaning than can be conveyed in just two or three words. Crisis stage one is 'Trust versus Mistrust', which is easier to understand than some of the others. Stage four 'Industry versus Inferiority' is a little trickier. You could say instead 'usefulness versus uselessness' in more modern common language. Erikson later refined 'Industry' to 'Industriousness', which probably conveys a fuller meaning. See the more detailed crisis stages descriptions below for a clearer understanding.

Successful passage through each stage is dependent on *striking the right balance between the conflicting extremes* rather than entirely focusing on (or being guided towards) the 'ideal' or 'preferable' extreme in each crisis. In this respect Erikson's theory goes a long way to explaining why too much of anything is not helpful for developing a well-balanced personality. A well-balanced positive experience during each stage develops a corresponding *'basic virtue'* (or 'basic strength - a helpful personality development), each of which enables a range of other related emotional and psychological strengths. For example passing successfully through the Industry versus Inferiority crisis (stage four, between 6-12 years of age for most people) produces the 'basic psychosocial virtue' of 'competence' (plus related strengths such as 'method', skills, techniques, ability to work with processes and collaborations, etc). More detail is under 'Basic virtues'.

Where passage through a crisis stage is less successful (in other words not well-balanced, or worse still, psychologically damaging) then to a varying extent the personality acquires an unhelpful emotional or psychological tendency, which corresponds to one of the two opposite extremes of the crisis concerned. Neglect and failure at any stage is problematical, but so is too much emphasis on the apparent 'good' extreme. For example unsuccessful experiences during the Industry versus Inferiority crisis would produce a tendency towards being overly focused on learning and work, or the opposite tendency towards uselessness and apathy. Describing these unhelpful outcomes, Erikson later introduced the terms *'maladaptation'* (overly adopting 'positive' extreme) and *'malignancy'* (adopting the 'negative' extreme). More detail is under 'Maladaptations' and 'Malignancies'. In the most extreme cases the tendency can amount to serious mental problems.

Eriksson's Psychosocial Crisis Stages—Meanings and Interpretations

Erikson used particular words to represent each psychosocial crisis. As ever, single words can be misleading and rarely convey much meaning. Here is more explanation of what lies behind these terms. Erikson reinforced these crisis explanations with a perspective called 'psychosocial modalities', which in the earlier stages reflect Freudian theory, and which are paraphrased below. They are not crucial to the model, but they do provide a useful additional viewpoint.

'psychosocial crisis'/ 'psychosocial modality'	meaning and interpretation
1. Trust v Mistrust To get' To give in return' (To receive and to give in return. Trust is reciprocal – maybe karma even..)	The infant will develop a healthy balance between trust and mistrust if fed and cared for and not over-indulged or over-protected. Abuse or neglect or cruelty will destroy trust and foster mistrust. Mistrust increases a person's resistance to risk-exposure and exploration. "Once bitten twice shy" is an apt analogy. On the other hand, if the infant is insulated from all and any feelings of surprise and normality, or unfailingly indulged, this will create a false sense of trust amounting to sensory distortion, in other words a failure to appreciate reality. Infants who grow up to trust are more able to hope and have faith that 'things will generally be okay'. This crisis stage incorporates Freud's psychosexual Oral stage, in which the infant's crucial

'psychosocial crisis'/ 'psychosocial modality'	meaning and interpretation
	relationships and experiences are defined by oral matters, notably feeding and relationship with mum. Erikson later shortened 'Basic Trust v Basic Mistrust' to simply Trust v Mistrust, especially in tables and headings.
2. Autonomy v Shame & Doubt To hold on'To let go' (To direct behaviour outward or be retentive. Of course very Freudian...)	Autonomy means self-reliance. This is independence of thought, and a basic confidence to think and act for oneself. Shame and Doubt mean what they say, and obviously inhibit self-expression and developing one's own ideas, opinions and sense of self. Toilet and potty training is a significant part of this crisis, as in Freud's psychosexual Anal stage, where parental reactions, encouragement and patience play an important role in shaping the young child's experience and successful progression through this period. The significance of parental reaction is not limited to bottoms and pooh - it concerns all aspects of toddler exploration and discovery while small children struggle to find their feet - almost literally - as little people in their own right. The 'terrible twos' and 'toddler tantrums' is a couple of obvious analogies which represent these internal struggles and parental battles. The parental balancing act is a challenging one, especially since parents themselves have to deal with their own particular psychosocial crisis, and of course deal with the influence of their own emotional triggers which were conditioned when they themselves passed through earlier formative crisis stages. What are the odds that whenever a parent berates a child, "That's dirty.." it will be an echo from their own past experience at this very stage?

'psychosocial crisis'/ 'psychosocial modality'	meaning and interpretation
3. Initiative v Guilt To make (= going after)"To "make like" (= playing)'(To make and complete things, and to make things together. To pursue ideas, plans)	Initiative is the capability to devise actions or projects, and a confidence and belief that it is okay to do so, even with a risk of failure or making mistakes. Guilt means what it says, and in this context is the feeling that it is wrong or inappropriate to instigate something of one's own design. Guilt results from being admonished or believing that something is wrong or likely to attract disapproval. Initiative flourishes when adventure and game-playing is encouraged, irrespective of how daft and silly it seems to the grown-up in charge. Suppressing adventure and experimentation, or preventing young children doing things for themselves because of time, mess or a bit of risk will inhibit the development of confidence to initiate, replacing it instead with an unhelpful fear of being wrong or unapproved. The fear of being admonished or accused of being stupid becomes a part of the personality. "If I don't initiate or stick my neck out I'll be safe.." (from feeling guilty and bad). Parents, careers and older siblings have a challenge to get the balance right between giving young children enough space and encouragement so as to foster a sense of purpose and confidence, but to protect against danger, and also to enable a sensible exposure to trail and error, and to the consequences of mistakes, without which an irresponsible or reckless tendency can develop. This crisis stage correlates with Freud's psychosexual Phallic stage, characterised by a perfectly natural interest in genitals, where babies come from,

'psychosocial crisis'/ 'psychosocial modality'	meaning and interpretation
	and as Freud asserted, an attachment to the opposite sex parent, and the murky mysteries of the Oedipus Complex, Penis Envy and Castration Anxiety, about which further explanation and understanding is not critical to appreciating Erikson's theory. What's more essential is to recognize that children of this age are not wicked or bad or naughty, they are exploring and
4. Industry v Inferiority' To make (= going after)'To "make like" and complete things, and to make things together' (To initiate projects or ideas, and to collaborate and cooperate with others to produce something.)	Industry here refers to purposeful or meaningful activity. It's the development of competence and skills, and a confidence to use a 'method', and is a crucial aspect of school years experience. Erikson described this stage as a sort of 'entrance to life'. This correlates with Freud's psychosexual Latency stage, when sexual motives and concerns are largely repressed while the young person concentrates on work and skills development. A child who experiences the satisfaction of achievement - of anything positive - will move towards successful negotiation of this crisis stage. A child who experiences failure at school tasks and work, or worse still who is denied the opportunity to discover and develop their own capabilities and strengths and unique potential, quite naturally is prone to feeling inferior and useless. Engaging with others and using tools or technology are also important aspects of this stage. It is like a rehearsal for being productive and being valued at work in later life. Inferiority is feeling useless; unable to contribute, unable to cooperate or work in a team to create something, with the low self-esteem that accompanies such feelings.Erikson knew

'psychosocial crisis'/ 'psychosocial modality'	meaning and interpretation
	this over fifty years ago. How is it that the people in charge of children's education still fail to realise this? Develop the child from within. Help them to find and excel at what they are naturally good at, and then they will achieve the sense of purpose and industry on which everything else can then be built.
5. Identity v Role Confusion' To be oneself (or not to be)" To share being oneself'(To be yourself and to share this with others. Affirmation or otherwise of how you see yourself.)	Identity means essentially how a person sees themselves in relation to their world. It's a sense of self or individuality in the context of life and what lies ahead. Role Confusion is the negative perspective - an absence of identity - meaning that the person cannot see clearly or at all who they are and how they can relate positively with their environment. This stage coincides with puberty or adolescence, and the reawakening of the sexual urge whose dormancy typically characterises the previous stage. Young people struggle to belong and to be accepted and affirmed, and yet also to become individuals. In itself this is a big dilemma, aside from all the other distractions and confusions experienced at this life stage. Erikson later replaced the term 'Role Confusion' with 'Identity Diffusion'. In essence they mean the same.
6. Intimacy v Isolation' To lose and find oneself in another' (Reciprocal love for and with another person.)	Intimacy means the process of achieving relationships with family and marital or mating partner(s). Erikson explained this stage also in terms of sexual mutuality - the giving and receiving of physical and emotional connection, support, love, comfort, trust, and all the other elements

'psychosocial crisis'/ 'psychosocial modality'	meaning and interpretation
	that we would typically associate with healthy adult relationships conducive to mating and child-rearing. There is a strong reciprocal feature in the intimacy experienced during this stage - giving and receiving - especially between sexual or marital partners. Isolation conversely means being and feeling excluded from the usual life experiences of dating and mating and mutually loving relationships. This logically is characterised by feelings of loneliness, alienation, social withdrawal or non-participation.Erikson also later correlated this stage with the Freudian Genitality sexual stage, which illustrates the difficulty in equating Freudian psychosexual theory precisely to Erikson's model. There is a correlation but it is not an exact fit.
7. Generativity v Stagnation'To make be''To take care of' (Unconditional, non-reciprocating care of one's children, or other altruistic outlets)	Generativity derives from the word generation, as in parents and children, and specifically the unconditional giving that characterises positive parental love and care for their offspring. Erikson acknowledged that this stage also extends to other productive activities - work and creativity for example - but given his focus on childhood development, and probably the influence of Freudian theory, Erikson's analysis of this stage was strongly oriented towards parenting. Generativity potentially extends beyond one's own children, and also to all future generations, which gives the model ultimately a very modern globally responsible perspective. Positive outcomes from this crisis stage depend on contributing positively and

'psychosocial crisis'/ 'psychosocial modality'	meaning and interpretation
	unconditionally. We might also see this as an end of self-interest. Having children is not a prerequisite for Generativity, just as being a parent is no guarantee that Generativity will be achieved. Caring for children is the common Generativity scenario, but success at this stage actually depends on giving and caring - putting something back into life, to the best of one's capabilities. Stagnation is an extension of intimacy which turns inward in the form of self-interest and self-absorption. It's the disposition that represents feelings of selfishness, self-indulgence, greed, lack of interest in young people and future generations, and the wider world. Erikson later used the term 'Self-Absorption' instead of 'Stagnation' and then seems to have settled in later work with the original 'Stagnation'. Stagnation and/or Self-Absorption result from not having an outlet or opportunity for contributing to the good or growth of children and others, and potentially to the wider world.
8. Integrity v Despair 'To be, through having been To face not being' (To be peaceful and satisfied with one's life and efforts, and to be accepting that life will end.)	This is a review and closing stage. The previous stage is actually a culmination of one's achievement and contribution to descendents, and potentially future generations everywhere. Later Erikson dropped the word 'Ego' (from 'Ego Integrity') and extended the whole term to 'Integrity v Disgust and Despair'. He also continued to use the shorter form 'Integrity v Despair'.

'psychosocial crisis'/ 'psychosocial modality'	meaning and interpretation
	Integrity means feeling at peace with oneself and the world. No regrets or recriminations. The linking between the stages is perhaps clearer here than anywhere: people are more likely to look back on their lives positively and happily if they have left the world a better place than they found it - in whatever way, to whatever extent. There lies Integrity and acceptance. Despair and/or 'Disgust' (*i.e.*, ejective denial, or 'sour grapes' feeling towards what life might have been) represent the opposite disposition: feelings of wasted opportunities, regrets, wishing to be able to turn back the clock and have a second chance. This stage is a powerful lens through which to view one's life—even before old age is reached. To bring this idea to life look at the 'obituaries' exercise. Erikson had a profound interest in humanity and society's well-being in general. This crisis stage highlights the issue very meaningfully. Happily these days for many people it's often possible to put something back, even in the depths of despair. When this happens people are effectively rebuilding wreckage from the previous stage, which is fine.

Eriksson's Basic Psychosocial Virtues or Strengths (positive outcomes)

The chart below identifies the *'basic psychosocial virtues'*—and related strengths—which result from successfully passing through each crisis. Erikson described success as a 'favourable ratio' (between the two extremes) at each crisis stage. A basic virtue is not the result of simply achieving the positive extreme of each crisis. Basic virtue is attained by a helpful balance, albeit towards the 'positive', between the two extremes. Helpfully balanced experience leads to positive growth.

Chief life stage issues and relationships are also re-stated as a reminder as to when things happen. 'Basic psychological virtue' and 'basic virtue' (same thing), are Erikson's terminology. Erikson identified one *basic virtue,* plus another virtue (described below a 'secondary virtue') for each stage. At times he referred to 'basic virtues' as 'basic strengths'. A bit confusing, but the main point is that based on what observed for each stage he identified one clear basic virtue and one secondary virtue. From this he was able to (and we can too - he encouraged people to do so) extrapolate other related strengths. Bear in mind also that the first disposition in each crisis is also inevitably a related strength that comes from successfully experiencing each stage. Erikson recognised this by later referring to the first disposition (e.g., Trust, Autonomy, etc) as an 'Adaptive Strength'.

Basic Virtues and Other Strengths

crisis including adaptive strength	basic virtue & secondary virtue (and related strengths)	life stage/ relationships/ issues
1. Trust v Mistrust	**Hope & Drive** (faith, inner calm, grounding, basic feeling that everything will be okay - enabling exposure to risk, a trust in life and self and others, inner resolve and strength in the face of uncertainty and risk)	infant / mother/ feeding and being comforted, teething, sleeping
2. **Autonomy v Shame & Doubt**	**Willpower & Self-Control** (self-determination, self-belief, self-reliance, confidence in self to decide things, having a voice, being one's own person, persis-	toddler / parents / bodily functions, toilet training, muscular control, walking

crisis including adaptive strength	basic virtue & secondary virtue (and related strengths)	life stage/ relationships/ issues
	tence, self-discipline, independence of thought, responsibility, judgement)	
3. **Initiative v Guilt**	**Purpose & Direction** (sense of purpose, decision-making, working with and leading others, initiating projects and ideas, courage to instigate, ability to define personal direction and aims and goals, able to take initiative and appropriate risks)	preschool/family/ exploration and discovery, adventure and play
4. **Industry v Inferiority**	**Competence & Method** (making things, producing results, applying skills and processes productively, feeling valued and capable of contributing, ability to apply method and process in pursuit of ideas or objectives, confidence to seek and respond to challenge and learning, active busy productive outlook)	schoolchild / school, teachers, friends, neighbourhood / achievement and accomplishment
5. Identity v Role Confusion	**Fidelity & Devotion** (self-confidence and self-esteem necessary to freely associate with people and ideas based on merit, loyalty, social and interpersonal integrity, discretion, personal standards and dignity, pride and personal identity, seeing useful personal role(s) and purpose(s) in life)	adolescent / peers, groups, influences/ resolving identity and direction, becoming a grown-up
6. Intimacy v Isolation	**Love & Affiliation** (capacity to give and receive love - emotionally and physically, connectivity with others, socially and inter-personally comfortable, ability to form honest recipro-	young adult / lovers, friends, work connections/ intimate relationships, work and social life

crisis including adaptive strength	basic virtue & secondary virtue (and related strengths)	life stage/ relationships/ issues
	cating relationships and friendships, capacity to bond and commit with others for mutual satisfaction—for work and personal life, reciprocity—give and take - towards good)	
7. Generativity v Stagnation	**Care & Production** (giving unconditionally in support of children and/or for others, community, society and the wider world where possible and applicable, altruism, contributing for the greater good, making a positive difference, building a good legacy, helping others through their own crisis stages	mid-adult/ children, community / 'giving back', helping, contributing
8. Integrity v Despair	**Wisdom & Renunciation** (calmness, tolerance, appropriate emotional detachment - non-projection, no regrets, peace of mind, non-judge mental, spiritual or universal reconciliation, acceptance of inevitably departing)	late adult / society, the world, life / meaning and purpose, life achievements, acceptance

Eriksson and Maslow Correlations?

As an aside, there are significant parallels between the growth outcomes of the Erikson psychosocial model, and the growth aspects *Maslow's Hierarchy of Needs.* It's not a precise fit obviously because the Erikson and Maslow perspectives are different, but the correlations are clear and fascinating. Erikson separately listed a series of 'Related Elements of Social Order' within his psychosocial model, which although quite obscure in this context, might aid the comparison. You might have your own views on this. For what it's worth here's mine:

life stage/relationships/ issues	crisis	virtue outcomes	Erikson's 'related elements of social order'	Maslow Hierarchy of Needs stage - primary correlation
infant/mother/feeding and being comforted, teething, sleeping	1. Trust v Mistrust	Hope & Drive	'cosmic order'	**biological & physiological**
toddler/parents/ bodily functions, toilet training, muscular control, walking	2. Autonomy v Shame & Doubt	Willpower & Self-Control	'law and order'	**safety**
preschool/family/ exploration and discovery, adventure and play	3. Initiative v Guilt	Purpose & Direction	'ideal proto-types'	**belonging-ness & love**
schoolchild/school, teachers, friends, neighbourhood/ achievement and accomplishment	4. Industry v Inferiority	Competence & Method	'technological elements'	**esteem**
adolescent/peers, groups, influences/ resolving identity and direction, becoming a grown-up	5. Identity v Role Confusion	Fidelity & Devotion	'ideological perspectives'	**esteem**
young adult / lovers, friends, work connections/ intimate relationships, work and social life	6. Intimacy v Isolation	Love & Affiliation	'patterns of cooperation and competition'	**esteem**
mid-adult/ children, community/ 'giving back', helping, contributing	7. Generativity v Stagnation	Care & Production	'currents of education and training'	**self-actualisation**
late adult / society, the world, life / meaning and purpose, life achievements, acceptance	8. Integrity v Despair	Wisdom & Renunciation	'wisdom'	**self-actualisation**

N.B. I'm not suggesting a direct fit between Erikson's and Maslow's models. Rather, this simply puts the two perspectives alongside each other to show how similar aspects could inter-relate. Judge for yourself. We might also use the Erikson model to help explain what happens in Maslow's theory when a particular trauma sweeps away a part of someone's life (perhaps due to redundancy, divorce, social exclusion, bankruptcy, homelessness), which causes the person to revisit certain needs and internal conflicts (crises) which were once satisfied earlier but are no longer met. According to both Erikson's and Maslow's theories, anyone can find themselves revisiting and having to resolve needs (or crisis feelings or experiences) from earlier years.

Eriksson's Model—Maladaptations and Malignancies (negative outcomes)

Later Erikson developed clearer ideas and terminology - notably 'Maladaptations' and 'Malignancies' - to represent the negative outcomes arising from an unhelpful experience through each of the crisis stages. In crude modern terms these negative outcomes might be referred to as 'baggage', which although somewhat unscientific, is actually a very apt metaphor, since people tend to carry with them through life the psychological outcomes of previously unhelpful experiences. Psychoanalysis, the particular therapeutic science from which Erikson approached these issues, is a way to help people understand where the baggage came from, and thereby to assist the process of dumping it.

To an extent these negative outcomes can also arise from repeating or revisiting a crisis, or more realistically the essential aspects of a crisis, since we don't actually regress to a younger age, instead we revisit the experiences and feelings associated with earlier life. This chart is laid out with the crisis in the centre to aid appreciation that 'maladaptations' develop from tending towards the extreme of the first ('positive') disposition in each crisis, and 'malignancies' develop from tending towards the extreme of the second ('negative') disposition in each crisis. A maladaptation could be seen as 'too much of a good thing'. A malignancy could be seen as not enough.

Maladaptations and Malignancies

Maladaptation	Crisis	Malignancy
Sensory Distortion (later Sensory Maladjustment)	Trust v Mistrust	Withdrawal
Impulsivity (later Shameless Willfulness)	Autonomy v Shame/Doubt	Compulsion
Ruthlessness	Initiative v Guilt	Inhibition
Narrow Virtuosity	Industry v Inferiority	Inertia
Fanaticism	Identity v Role Confusion	Repudiation
Promiscuity	Intimacy v Isolation	Exclusivity
Overextension	Generativity v Stagnation	Rejectivity
Presumption	Integrity v Despair	Disdain

Erikson was careful to choose words for the maladaptations and malignancies which convey a lot of meaning and are very symbolic of the emotional outcomes that are relevant to each stage. In each case the maladaptation or malignancy corresponds to an extreme extension of the relevant crisis disposition (for example, 'Withdrawal' results from an extreme extension of 'Mistrust'). Thinking about this helps to understand what these outcomes entail, and interestingly helps to identify the traits in people - or oneself - when you encounter the behavioural tendency concerned.

Malignancies and maladaptations can manifest in various ways. Here are examples, using more modern and common language, to help understand and interpret the meaning and possible attitudes, tendencies, behaviours, etc., within the various malignancies and malapdations. In each case the examples can manifest as more extreme mental difficulties, in which case the terms would be more extreme too. These examples are open to additional interpretation and are intended to be a guide, not scientific certainties. Neither do these examples suggest that anyone experiencing any of these behavioural tendencies is suffering from mental problems. Erikson never established any absolute measurement of emotional difficulty or tendency as to be defined as a malignancy or maladaptation.

In truth each of us is subject to emotional feelings and extremes of various sorts, and it is always a matter of opinion as to what actually constitutes a problem. All people possess a degree of maladaptation or malignancy from each crisis experience. Not to do so would not be human, since none of us is perfect. It's always a question of degree. It's also a matter of understanding our weaknesses, maybe understanding where they come from too, and thereby better understanding how we might become stronger, more productive and happier.

Maladaptations and Malignancies—Examples and Interpretations

examples	maladaptation	crisis	malignancy	examples
unrealistic, spoilt, deluded	Sensory Distortion	Trust v Mistrust	Withdrawal	neurotic, depressive, afraid
reckless, inconsi-derate, thoughtless	Impulsivity	Autonomy v Shame/Doubt	Compulsion	anal, constrained, self-limiting
exploitative, uncaring, dis-passionate	Ruthlessness	Initiative v Guilt	Inhibition	risk-averse, unadventurous
workaholic, obsessive specialist	Narrow Virtuosity	Industry v Inferiority	Inertia	lazy, apathetic, purposeless
self-impor-tant, extremist	Fanaticism	Identity v Role Confusion	Repudiation	socially disconnected, cut-off
sexually needy, vulnerable	Promiscuity	Intimacy v Isolation	Exclusivity	loner, cold, self-contained
do-gooder, busy-body, meddling	Overextension	Generativity v Stagnation	Rejectivity	disinterested, cynical
conceited, pompous, arrogant	Presumption	Integrity v Despair	Disdain	miserable, unfulfilled, blaming

Eriksson's Terminology

This section explains how some of the model's terminology altered as Erikson developed his theory, and is not crucial to understanding the model at a simple level. Erikson was continually refining and re-evaluating his psychosocial theory, and he encouraged his readers and followers to do likewise. This developmental approach enabled the useful extension of the model to its current format. Some of what is summarised here did not initially appear clearly in Childhood and Society in 1950, which marked the establishment of the basic theory, not its completion. Several aspects of Erikson's theory were clarified in subsequent books decades later, including work focusing on old age by Joan Erikson, Erik's wife and collaborator, notably in the 1996 revised edition of The Life Cycle Completed: A Review. The Eriksons' refinements also involved alterations - some would say complications - to the terminology, which (although presumably aiming for scientific precision) do not necessarily aid understanding, especially at a basic working level. For clarity therefore this page sticks mostly with Erikson's original 1950 and other commonly used terminology. Basic Trust v Basic Mistrust (1950) is however shortened here to Trust v Mistrust, and Ego Integrity (1950) is shortened to Integrity, because these seem to be more consistent Erikson preferences. The terms used on this page are perfectly adequate, and perhaps easier too, for grasping what the theory means and making use of it. Here are the main examples of alternative terminology that Erikson used in later works to describe the crisis stages and other aspects, which will help you recognise and understand their meaning if you see them elsewhere.

- Erikson used the terms 'syntonic' and 'dystonic' to describe the contrary dispositions and effects within each crisis stage - 'syntonic' being the 'positive' first-listed factor (e.g., Trust) and 'dystonic' being the 'negative' second-listed word (e.g., Mistrust). Again realise that a balance between syntonic and dystonic tendencies is required for healthy outcomes. Extreme tendency in either direction is not helpful. Syntonic extremes equate to maladaptations. Dystonic extremes equate to malignancies. The words syntonic and dystonic outside of Erikson's theory have quite specific scientific medical meanings which are not easy to equate to Erikson's essential ideas. Syntonic conventionally refers to a high degree of emotional response to one's environment; dystonic conventionally refers to abnormal muscular responsiveness. See what I mean?.. neither literal definition particularly aids understanding of Erikson's theory and as such they are not very helpful in using the model.

- Erikson later used 'Adaptive Strength' as a firm description of the first disposition in each crisis, e.g., Trust, Autonomy and Initiative. He used the description loosely early in his work but seems to have settled on it as a firm heading in later work, (notably in Vital Involvement in Old Age, 1986).
- 'Basic Virtues' Erikson also called 'Basic Strengths' (the word 'basic' generally identified the single main virtue or strength that potentially arose from each crisis, which would be accompanied by various other related strengths).
- Erikson (or maybe Joan Erikson) later used the term 'Antipathy' as an alternative for 'Malignancy' (being the negative tendency towards the second resulting from unsuccessful experience during a crisis stage).
- 'Sensory Distortion' was later referred to as 'Sensory Maladjustment', being the maladaptive tendency arising at stage one (Trust v Mistrust).
- 'Impulsivity' he later changed to 'Shameless Willfulness', being the maladaptive tendency arising at stage two (Autonomy v Shame & Doubt)

- Erikson generally used the simpler 'Trust v Mistrust' instead of 'Basic Trust v Basic Mistrust' which first appeared in the 1950 model.
- Erikson later refined 'Industry' to 'Industriousness'.
- Erikson later referred to 'Role Confusion' as 'Identity Diffusion' and 'Identity Confusion'.
- He later referred to 'Intimacy' also as 'Intimacy and Distantiation'. (Distantiation means the ability to bring objectivity - emotional detachment - to personal decision-making.)
- 'Ego Integrity' he also simplified at times to simply 'Integrity'.
- 'Stagnation' was later shown alternatively as 'Self-Absorption', and later still reverted to 'Stagnation'.
- At times he extended 'Despair' to 'Despair and Disgust' (Disgust here being a sort of 'sour grapes' reaction or rejective denial).

In conclusion

Erikson's psychosocial theory very powerful for self-awareness and improvement, and for teaching and helping others. While Erikson's model emphasises the sequential significance of the eight character-forming crisis stages, the concept also asserts that humans continue to change and develop throughout their lives, and that personality is not exclusively formed during early childhood years. This is a helpful and optimistic idea, and many believe it is realistic too. It is certainly a view that greatly assists encouraging oneself and others to see the future as an opportunity for positive change and development, instead of looking back with blame and regret.

The better that people come through each crisis, the better they will tend to deal with what lies ahead, but this is not to say that all is lost and never to be recovered if a person has had a negative experience during any particular crisis stage.

Lessons can be revisited successfully when they recur, if we recognise and welcome them. Everyone can change and grow, no matter what has gone before. And as ever, understanding why we are like we are - gaining meaningful self-awareness - is always a useful and important step forward. Erikson's theory, along with many other concepts featured on this website, helps to enable this meaningful understanding and personal growth.

Erikson's psychosocial theory should be taught to everyone - especially to school children, teachers and parents - it's certainly accessible enough, and would greatly assist all people of all ages to understand the connections between life experiences and human behaviour - and particularly how grown-ups can help rather than hinder children's development into rounded emotionally mature people. Erikson was keen to improve the way children and young people are taught and nurtured, and it would be appropriate for his ideas to be more widely known and used in day-to-day life, beyond the clinical and counselling professions. Hopefully this page explains Erikson's psychosocial theory in reasonable simple terms. I'm always open to suggestions of improvements, especially for a challenging and potent area like this one. I recommend for more detail you see the wonderful materials created by Professor George Boeree of the Shippensburg (Pennsylvania) University Psychology Department, and specifically *George Boeree's Erikson theory explanation.* Or read any of Erikson's books - they are very accessible and rich in ideas, and they do have a strong resonance with much of what we face in modern life.

Erik Eriksson—Biography

Erik Homburger Erikson (1902-94) was born in Frankfurt-am-Main Germany on 15 June 1902 to a young Danish Jewish woman, Karla Abrahamsen. His natural father departed before the birth, and his mother subsequently married Dr Theodor Homberger, Erik's paediatrician. Erik changed his surname later in life, seemingly on becoming an American citizen. A degree of uncertainty about personal identity and direction apparently characterised Erik's childhood and early adult years - not surprisingly given his circumstances - which reflected and perhaps helped inspire his life work.

After wandering and working around Europe as an artist, Erikson came to psychoanalysis almost by accident. Around 1927 aged 25 he took a teaching job at an experimental school for American children in Vienna run by psychoanalyst Dorothy Burlingham (daughter of New York jeweller Charles Tiffany incidentally - she initially came to Vienna for psychoanalysis). This appointment was pivotal: it introduced Erikson to Montessori education methods, to psychoanalysis, to Anna Freud (lifelong friend and collaborator of Dorothy Burlingham), and also to the Vienna Psychoanalytic Society, Sigmund Freud's centre of psychoanalytical excellence. The work and teachings of Sigmund Freud and daughter Anna were to prove hugely significant in the development of Erikson's own ideas and direction, and all from an inconspicuous teaching appointment.

Erikson's early specialisation was child analysis, in which his interest and research grew following his emigration to the USA in 1933, where he also engaged in clinical work and teaching at Harvard, Yale, and later Berkeley California. Erik Erikson's early work focused chiefly on testing and extending Freudian theory in relation to the effect of social and cultural factors upon human psychology, with a strong emphasis on how society affects childhood and development. This research entailed detailed anthropological studies of children in societies, notably conducted in 1938 with the Oglala Lakota (Sioux) and Yurok Native American people. These experiences especially helped Erikson to realise that Freudian ideas lacked vital social dimensions, and provided a key for his 'biopsychosocial' perspective.

He subsequently moved to the University of California, continuing his focus on child welfare, and also practiced at the San Francisco Veterans Hospital treating trauma and mental illness. When McCarthy demanded California academics sign the 'loyalty oath' in 1950, Erikson moved to Massachusetts, where he taught and worked for ten years until moving to Harvard. He retired from clinical practice, but not from research and writing, in 1970, back to Massachusetts, and died in 1994. Erik's Canadian wife Joan M Erikson, whom he met and married in Vienna, was also keenly interested and expert in the life stages theory and its application to childhood development and psychoanalysis. She collaborated in Erikson's clinical and teaching work and in the development and writing of his ideas too. She died in 1997, three years after her husband. They had two sons and a daughter.

Erikson's first and arguably most important book, Childhood and Society, was published in 1950, in which he first explained his eight stage theory of human development, and incidentally also established the concept of the 'identity crisis' in adolescence. Later books reflected his interest in humanistic and society perspectives and his own passage through later life stages, and included Young Man Luther (1958), Identity and the Life Cycle (1959), Insight and Responsibility (1964), Identity: Youth and Crisis (1968), Gandhi's Truth (1970) - which won the Pulizter Prize, and Dimensions of a New Identity (1974). Erickson's book The Life Cycle Completed: A Review (1982) was revised in 1996 by Joan Erikson in which she extended the stages of old age within the life cycle model. The book Vital Involvement in Old Age (1989), which revisited people and life stages first studied forty years earlier, was jointly written with Joan Erikson and Helen Kivnik.

Index

I